English # Heritage
Book of
Abbeys and Priories

Glyn Coppack

B. T. Batsford Ltd/English Heritage
London

*This book is dedicated to
nameless English monks and nuns
without whose lives of prayer and
meditation it would not have been
possible to write*

Typeset by Lasertext, Stretford, Manchester
and printed
by
The Bath Press, Bath

for the publishers
B. T. Batsford Ltd
4 Fitzhardinge Street
London W1H 0AH

ISBN 0 7134 6308 2 (cased)
0 7134 6309 0 (limp)

6003736955

Contents

Illustrations

Colour plates

Preface

There were not many parts of medieval England that did not have a local abbey or priory; indeed monastic life was as old as English christianity itself. Monks and nuns were a part of everyday life, though they set themselves apart from society to praise God in elaborate and costly buildings. They were supported in their religious life by landed estates, the gifts of founders and patrons, and gifts from ordinary people. They supported a way of life which is now foreign to us. Although monastic life is no longer an integral part of our society, the remains of medieval religious life are still with us, in many of our cathedrals and parish churches, in surviving buildings, ruins, and even in place names. After parish churches monastic remains comprise the greatest collection of surviving medieval architecture. What survives today is a small portion of what we have lost since all abbeys and priories were suppressed in the sixteenth century, but it is a significant portion, which can tell us a great deal if it is examined carefully.

It has become traditional to look at monasteries through the eyes and mind of the historian or architect, with common factors becoming lost in the discussion of the many different orders of religious that populated the English monasteries and their buildings. Whilst the differences between orders were felt very keenly by the orders concerned time has gradually erased all but the most obvious of them and, to my mind, made it much easier to appreciate monasticism for what it was, the most remarkable aspect of a developing church. In this book I am therefore more interested in common factors than radical differences, and my approach is thematic rather than typological. As a result, the remarkable degree of common ground between worldly Benedictine and austere Carthusian, rich and poor, monk and nun, becomes apparent, restoring the links that earlier research has tended to obscure. Mine is not a voice crying in the wilderness: monastic studies are changing to appreciate the whole rather than the part, and this is my personal contribution to a developing field of study.

The skills required to understand the life of medieval monks and nuns – those of historian, theologian, architectural historian, historical geographer and archaeologist – are found in few people. In consequence, this review of monastic life through the eyes of an archaeologist has to borrow heavily from other disciplines, just as other specialists have to borrow the archaeological component to understand their own work. With so many monastic sites in England, it is impossible and unnecessary to describe them all for, though no two monastic sites are ever precisely alike, the differences are, on the whole, both minor and predictable. The sites I have chosen to describe are those that I know and love the best, and for this I make no apology. If I have omitted particular sites it should not imply that they are of any less significance than the ones I include, it is simply that the line had to be drawn somewhere and my personal bias is reflected in the choice between equals.

In writing this book, I have made free use of advice and information made available to me over the past 15 years by a great many people. My greatest debt of gratitude must be to the late Roy Gilyard-Beer and Stuart Rigold. If they were alive today they would recognize many of my statements as their own. I can only hope that they would approve of the way in which I have developed other lines of research that they originally suggested. More particularly, I have benefited from the ideas and arguments, both in print and unpublished, of Stuart Harrison, Stephen Moorhouse, Stuart

Wrathmell, Peter Fergusson, Susan Wright, Susan Hirst, David and Evelyn Baker, David Walsh, Judith Roebuck, Andrew Davison, Philip Rahtz, Richard Kemp, David Sherlock, Christopher Norton, Roberta Gilchrist, Jim Lang, Philip Mayes, Shirley Johnson, Peter Huggins, Jim Thorn and many others. Any errors of fact are my responsibility, not theirs, and any variation on the interpretation of other people's research is entirely my own.

Most of the line drawings in this book are the work of Miranda Schofield and Dawn Flower, others are the work of Philip Rahtz, Simon Hayfield, Judith Dobie, Jean Dowling, Denny Coppack and myself. Where these are taken from published drawings the original source is credited in the caption. Photographs, unless otherwise credited, are my own or from the English Heritage collection.

Glyn Coppack
Goxhill
St Lucy's Day, 1989

1

The archaeology of English monasteries

There were more than 1000 monasteries in medieval England, ranging from the small and inconsequential to the great and powerful. Some were only occupied for short periods before moving sites or combining with other communities, others were occupied for four or more centuries, some dating from well before the Norman conquest of 1066. Those that did not fall by the wayside were ruthlessly suppressed between 1536 and 1540, leaving only a pitiful number of surviving buildings, rather more broken ruins, and dispersed contents. No complete medieval monastery survives in England, though after parish churches they comprise the largest group of surviving medieval stone buildings. The concept of monastic life, once an integral part of our social history, is now foreign to us, and 'bare ruined choirs' are objects of fascination and mystery. Even the cathedrals and parish churches that survived the wreck of the dissolution have been physically altered to suit new liturgies. Elsewhere, stripped and quarried ruins are all that remain of institutions that were intended to last for ever as perpetual reminders of their founders' piety and communities' devotion. Some were destroyed so completely that the only indications of their existence are the earthworks that cover their buried foundations or spreads of rubble, tiles and pottery in the ploughed soil of arable fields. Others are lost below housing, with even their precise locations uncertain. Together, though, these thousand or so monasteries contain the evidence for the nature of monastic life in medieval England, and in their structural remains they show the aspirations, customs and economy of their long-dead inhabitants. The developing and careful study of their remains, using the skills of archaeology, the reading of their fabric, and the interpretation of their surviving documents, can now give a clear insight into their building, use, economy and communities.

There was no such thing as a typical monastery because the monastic movement was one of continuing reform and extension. From the early ninth century all medieval monks and nuns lived by the precepts of St Benedict, who compiled a rule for the monks of his abbey of Monte Casino in the early years of the sixth century. The followers of this rule became known as Benedictines and remained the predominant order of religion until the late tenth century. By this time, the Benedictine rule was found to be too easy for many groups, and the next two-and-a-half centuries saw the growth of many reform movements within the order, particularly those of the Cluniacs, the Savigniacs, and the Cistercians, all of whom lived enclosed lives. Each different rule observed its own particular customs, which were reflected in dress, liturgy, architecture, manuscripts, strictness of life and position in society. In every case, their buildings differed in details of planning and in the degree of decoration and fittings. In addition to the enclosed monks and nuns of these orders, a movement had grown up among bodies of clergy who served collegiate churches yet sought a similar form of monastic community. Bodies of canons banded together, living under a modified version of the Benedictine rule and precepts developed by St Augustine. From their rule, they became known as Augustinian canons, as austere as the fundamentalist Cistercians but living less enclosed lives and serving parish churches as well as their own monasteries. Other groups of canons and canonesses, the Premonstratensians and Gilbertines, developed their own rules, strongly influenced by the Cistercians. Again, their buildings varied according to their rule and liturgy.

All houses of canons, canonesses, monks,

nuns, and friars were established for a purpose: to house and sustain groups of religious who would pray for the souls of the founder and his descendants, and to provide them with a place of burial. They provided a home for those who chose to withdraw from the distractions of the world to serve God in a continuous round of prayer and devotion as part of an ordered community. A monastery therefore had to consist of a church, domestic buildings in which the community would live, a place for their burial, buildings to process their foodstuffs and agricultural estates to feed them and provide capital for building, a concept it is difficult to gain from the surviving buildings and ruins which tend to comprise only the nucleus of a once greater whole. In theory at least, monasteries should be self-sufficient, and for the most part they were, with farms and manors that exploited their estates.

Most monasteries were established in rural areas, often on marginal land, although a number were built in or just outside towns, often on the sites of preconquest monasteries. Some, like Battle Abbey or Bridlington Priory, established towns and markets at their gates, which were an important source of cash revenue, though like most they were supported primarily by agriculture. They formed an important element of the national economy, and in producing scholars and trained administrators provided the first civil servants. Their presidents enjoyed the rank of major landowners, an honour that carried responsibility for the administration of justice, the abbots of the greatest houses actually sitting in parliament. Their accumulated wealth and lands, coupled with their separation from an increasingly secular society, led to their downfall, in many ways marking the effective end of the Middle Ages in England. In little more than four years, Henry VIII and his chief minister, Thomas Cromwell, destroyed what had taken centuries to create. Their churches were dismantled, their cloisters turned into private houses or simply used as quarries, the contents dispersed or ruthlessly destroyed, and their lands sold off or added to the royal estates.

The origins of antiquarian interest

Interest in the cultural wealth of monasteries, their buildings, plate and libraries began before their destruction, when John Leland, the King's Antiquary, travelled the country in the 1520s. Leland found them to be treasure-houses without equal, and from his accounts it is possible to gauge the scale of loss that resulted from their suppression. His own claim in 1549 that he had 'conservid many good autors, the which other wise had beene like to have perischid' is palpably true. He was followed in little more than a decade by the Royal Commissioners of the *Valor Ecclesiasticus*, 1535. These commissioners were not charged with recording the cultural treasures of the monasteries; rather their task was to value them as real estate, for, since the king became Head of the Church in England, all church property had become a state asset. The commissioners were to list the lands and rents of each house (1); to survey and describe the buildings, particularly those with valuable lead roofs; and to list any debts. They were followed by other commissioners whose job was to assess the quality of monastic life, men like Richard Leyton, Thomas Legh, and Edward ApRice, whose motives might easily be questioned from the scurrilous and partisan reports they made. These surveys, the first stage in the destruction of monastic life, are the starting point for any study of monasteries in England and being government records, many have survived. They tell us a great deal about the buildings and their contents at the end of their life, and they present a good secular view of monastic life when it was still an integral part of everyday affairs. One particular survey made for the *Valor*, that of the poor Benedictine nunnery of Wilberfoss, has been used throughout this book to describe through contemporary eyes the precise nature of monastic buildings.

The first interest in suppressed monasteries became apparent during the second half of the sixteenth century and continued up to and beyond the Civil War. Following the wholesale destruction of monastic libraries and service books, antiquaries like Sir Robert Cotton and Edward Fairfax collected what remained, saving many chronicles, histories, collections of charters (colour plate 2), spiritual works and even service books. Some of the finest books had been reserved at the suppression for the royal libraries, but works of the quality of the Lindisfarne Gospels found their way into Cotton's collection, which ultimately became the nucleus of the British Museum library in 1753. More prosaically, the new owners of monastic estates retained the collections of

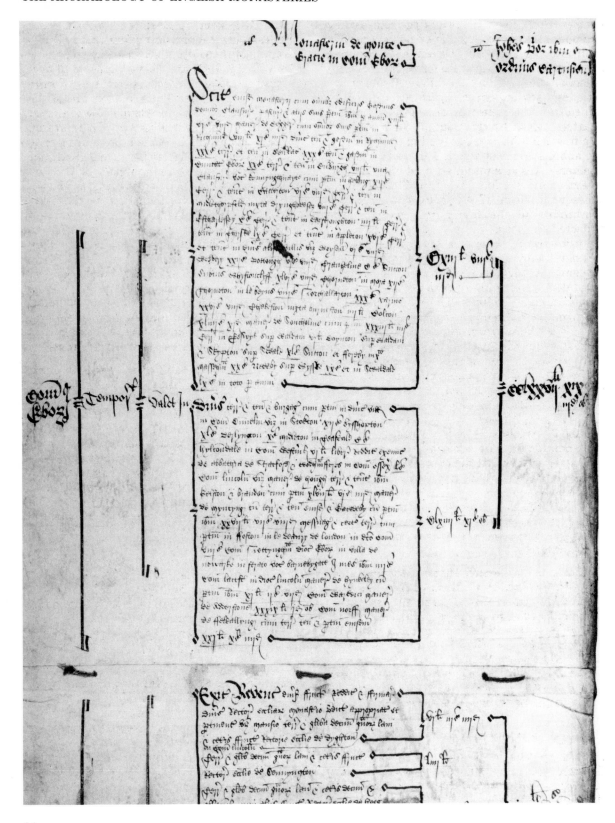

charters that proved the title to the estates they had bought, and protected these as jealously as their more recent deeds. Others were retained by agents of the government for identical reasons. The legal status of many former monastic land-holdings in the north could be ascertained from the collection of original monastic charters stored by the Council for the North in a tower on the precinct wall of York Abbey, the abbot's house of which became their headquarters. A sad consequence of the royalist defeat at the battle of Marston Moor and the subsequent siege of York in 1644 was the destruction of the tower and many of the collected charters.

Antiquarian interest in the muniments of defunct abbeys continued throughout the seventeenth century, exemplified by Sir William Dugdale, Garter King of Arms, who produced with ʿRoger Dodsworth the *Monasticon Anglicanum* in three volumes between 1655 and 1673. The *Monasticon*, the first synthesis of English monastic history, was compiled from transcriptions of documents recovered from the spoliation of the suppression that extended back to the eleventh century or before. Its timing was critical, coming in the recovery from the Civil War. Though the subject smacked of popery, the emphasis was on patronage, estates and individuals. For a nation in search of a non-partisan identity, the ruins and documents of the long-dead abbeys and priories provided a satisfactory outlet.

In the 1660s, John Aubrey, thinking back, no doubt, to the golden days before the Great Rebellion, described the remains of Waverley Abbey thus:

> The Abby is situated, though low, in a very good Air, and is as Romantick a Place as most I have seen. Here is a fine Rivulet runs under the House and fences one Side; but all the rest is wall'd. By the Lane are stately Rocks of Sand. Within the Walls of the Abbey are sixty acres: The Walls are very strong and chiefly of Ragge-Stones ten foot [3 m] high. Here also remain Walls of a fair *Church* the Walls of the *Cloyster* and some Part of

the Cloysters themselves, within and without are yet remaining: Within the Quadrangle of the Cloysters was a Pond, but now is a Marsh. Here was also a handsom Chapel (now a stable) larger than that at *Trinity* College in *Oxford*. The Windows are of the same Fashion as the Chapel Windows at Priory St *Mari'es* in *Wiltshire*. There are no Escutcheons or Monuments remaining only in the Parlour and chamber over it (built not long since) are some Roundels of Painted Glass, *viz. St Michael* fighting with the Devil, St *Dunstan* holding the *Devil* by the Nose with his Pincers; his Retorts, Crucibles, and Chemical Instruments about him with several others; but so exactly drawn as if they were done from a good modern Print. They are of about eight Inches [20 cm] Diameter. The *Hall* was very spacious and noble with a Row of Pillers in the middle and vaulted over Head. The very long Building with long narrow Windows, in all Probability, was the *Dormitory*. There are many more ruins.

Though Aubrey was an exceptional antiquary, the points he examined at Waverley identify the interest that was current in monastic sites: what remained, what it compared with, the possible identification of buildings, and the survival of heraldry and window glass.

Not only did the *Monasticon* encourage an academic interest in monastic ruins, but also they began to be recorded artistically as objects of wonder and curiosity for the first time. The first such venture was Daniel King's *Cathedral and Conventual Churches of England and Wales*, published in 1656, and using drawings by Thomas Johnson (2), a valuable indication of how much or how little had survived the first century after the suppression. From this beginning, a valuable series of drawings, paintings and prints continued well into the nineteenth century, recording with great clarity more recent losses of fabric.

Monastic sites in the eighteenth century

A more general interest in monastic sites grew in the second quarter of the eighteenth century, with the growing interest in medieval architecture that gave rise to the Gothick style of building typified by Horace Walpole's Strawberry Hill and by Viscount Camden's villa at Bayham Abbey (3). Bayham offered the chance to build a fashionable house on the site of a

1 *Part of the first membrane of the* Valor Ecclesiasticus *roll for Mount Grace Priory, showing the value of the house's estates in 1535 (Public Record Office).*

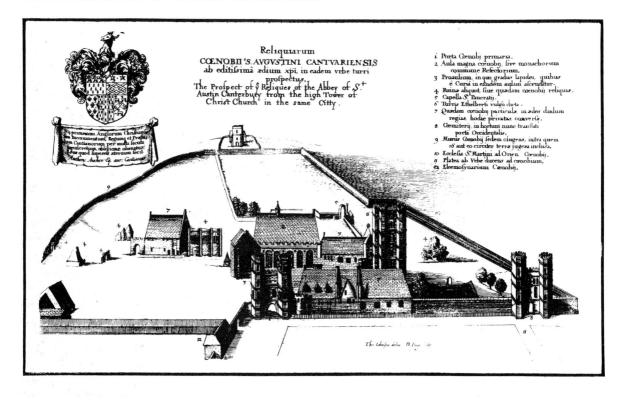

2 *The site of St Augustine's Abbey at Canterbury as it was in about 1650. Many of the buildings shown on this engraving still survive though the tower that marks the west end of the nave fell in 1822.*

real monastery, but the house was built in 1754 at the expense of the ruins, the thirteenth century roof being removed from the eastern part of the church that had survived as a barn (**4**) for reuse in the new house, walls demolished and new 'ruins' created to improve the melancholy aspect of the site.

Though there was a growing awareness of the value of monastic ruins, their survival was still very much a matter of luck. Indeed, the middle of the eighteenth century was a bad time for surviving fabric. Dr Stukeley observed of Bardney Abbey in 1753: 'Mr Rob. Banks gave me the following inscriptions on tombstones now under the turf at Bardney Abby. The abby is intirely demolished and was so when I saw it many years ago. 'Tis now a pasture, but the rubbish of the sacred structure has covered up the pavement of the church which they are now digging for the sake of the stones'. Though interest in ruins was to increase throughout the later eighteenth century, little was done to

preserve them as relics of the past. William Aislabie, when he added the extensive ruins of Fountains Abbey to his father's gardens at Studley Royal, felt no concern in removing those parts that got in the way of his garden scheme and increasing the dereliction of the site to improve his vista. Lord Scarborough's gardens at Sandbeck Park were reorganized by Lancelot 'Capability' Brown in 1774, the contract specifying that his design should accord with 'Poet's Feeling and Painter's Eye', the intention being to create an appropriately picturesque setting for the ruins of Roche Abbey. To achieve this, Brown demolished the greater part of the cloister buildings, an action that was even then seen as unnecessary vandalism. Until the site was excavated in the 1870s, the only visible ruins of Roche were the walls of the transepts and eastern arm of the church and small outcrops of masonry, for Brown chose to bury the greater part of the site below parterres that were removed only after the First World War.

A scholarly approach

The turn of the nineteenth century saw some improvement in the preservation of monastic ruins, however, as the value of the evidence

3 *The gothick villa built at Bayham Abbey by Viscount Camden in the 1750s.*

they contained became more widely appreciated. At Bayham, for instance, when Humphrey Repton was advising on the extension of Lord Camden's villa, William Wilkins was being consulted on the best means to preserve the ruins of the nave of the church. His advice – to rebuild missing buttresses in such a way as the new work could not be mistaken for old, using appropriate mortar – has a strangely modern ring to it. It marked the turning tide in the fortunes of monastic ruins.

Just as Lord Camden's work at Bayham was modified for a more subtle taste by Wilkins and Repton, the unscholarly 'gothick' of the 1740s and 1750s had given way to a true academic interest in medieval architecture by the last years of the century, reaching its peak in John Britton's studies of the great cathedral priory of Norwich (1817) and Bath Abbey (1825). The first half of the nineteenth century saw intense work done, principally on the surviving monastic churches, which were undergoing extensive 'restorations' to return them to an approximation of their original form. J. and C. Buckler produced a remarkable record of St Alban's Abbey in its parlous but untouched state in 1847. At the same time Robert Willis was subjecting Christchurch at Canterbury to a highly analytical survey, identifying breaks in building with surviving documentation to read the history of the monastery in its stones. Restoration and repair brought scaffolding, allowing scholars to have proper access to medieval fabric for the first time. This interest soon spread from surviving buildings to the more important ruins and monastic sites played a crucial role in the understanding of medieval architecture.

4 *Camden's removal of the thirteenth-century roof of the eastern part of the church at Bayham Abbey allowed the building to become a more romantic ruin much more in keeping with the tastes of the eighteenth century as this water-colour by James Lambert of 1785 shows.*

Archaeology and monastic sites

The scholarly interest in monasteries that was so well established by the first quarter of the nineteenth century did not stop at studying their architecture and the surviving document-ation. The next stage was to recover lost sites or details of surviving ruins by the developing techniques of archaeology. In 1790, John Mar-tin of Ripon had been inspired by Burton's *Monasticon Eboracense* to search the chapter-house at Fountains Abbey for the tombs of the abbots whose burial there had been recorded in the abbey's 'President Book'. Persuading the non-resident owner's gardener to clear the room out for him, he did indeed reveal many of the grave slabs he sought, as well as a 'very curious . . . pavement', and the bases of the col-umns that supported the vault. The vault itself, which had fallen, was simply barrowed out into the cloister where it remained until 1851, obscuring the bottom 2.2 m (7 ft) of the chapter-house façade. No plan was made or any note published, but Martin's exercise had demon-strated that excavation could be used to prove the evidence of medieval documents.

To search for burials was one thing; to reco-ver the plans of lost or buried buildings was another. The excavation of the church of Jer-vaulx Abbey, thoroughly demolished 1537–8 and buried below fallen debris, by John Cla-ridge, agent to the Earl of Ailesbury, between 1805 and 1807 followed his growing interest in the site, the gradual clearance of fallen debris and the repair of the ruins. Not only was the church cleared out to reveal its plan, fittings and elaborate floor tiles, it was also planned in detail (**colour plate 8**), an important development in the growing concept of monastic archaeology. Fallen architectural detail, though not recorded, was stacked along the lines of walls, which were reduced to a few courses above floor level, close to their original findspots where they can still be seen today. From these, the form of the lost superstructure can still be recovered. The chapter-house was also excavated to reveal the grave-markers of six abbots and to enable the re-erection of the fallen columns that had originally supported the vault (**colour plate 9**). Like Bayham and Roche, the intention was to develop the ruins at Jervaulx to form a feature in a landscaped park. The difference was that an appreciation of the abbey buildings and the layout of the precinct was allowed to influence the landscape

in a way that had previously not been considered. Jervaulx today is as important for its early nineteenth-century setting as it is for its late twelfth-century buildings.

In the 1820s, the wealthy Benedictine Abbey at York was excavated before a new museum was built on its site by the Yorkshire Philosophical Society, revealing substantial remains of the cloister ranges standing up to 2.4 m (8 ft) or more in height (**5**). Whilst the new museum building, of impeccable neo-classical design, was to occupy the site of the east range, such was the interest caused by the discovery that the excavators went on to examine the whole area of the claustral nucleus, producing in 1829 one of the earliest detailed plans of a monastic ruin. Though most of the site was subsequently reburied, the quality of record produced at the time of its excavation, coupled with the mass of fallen architectural detail recovered, enables the buildings to be reinterpreted today. Though the excavators were unable to resolve the building phases apparent in the walls they uncovered, it is clear that they realized they were dealing with many rebuildings and remodellings, a number of which were recorded in contemporary documents. This site gave the

5 *A view of the excavations of St Mary's Abbey, York, in 1828 by F. Nash which shows the partial demolition of the east range of the cloister buildings in advance of the construction of the Yorkshire Museum (York Minster Library).*

first indication of how complicated the archaeology of monastic sites could be and demonstrated the potential of buried sites, as both sources of architectural detail and confirmation of documented history. Martin Stapylton's excavation at Byland in about 1820 began as a search for the tomb of the founder Roger de Mowbray and became a hunt for capitals, corbels and other architectural elements, which were then removed to Myton Hall where they remain as garden ornaments. Similarly, Captain Chalonner's excavation in the church at Gisborough Priory in the 1840s led to the recovery of vast amounts of architectural detail, much of it found in place but sadly removed.

The reasons for nineteenth-century interest

Monasteries held a fascination for early Victorian society which sought to break free from eighteenth-century classicism and re-establish its medieval roots, a move led by both the Evangelical and the Anglo-Catholic wings of the Church of England. Abbeys rather than castles offered a tangible link with the medieval past that a highly motivated society could identify with: with piety, with patronage and with the newly-popularized Gothic architecture. Not all of society was interested – in 1816 Lord Yarborough bought the site of Thornton Abbey from his neighbour to prevent its continued quarrying for road stone. His son excavated the ruins up to 1835 and recovered much of the ground plan. In 1835 the sometime quarry was opened to the paying public with a paid Keeper of the Ruins. So popular did the site become that it even acquired its own railway station. Indeed, the increased mobility afforded to the general public by the railways in the second half of the nineteenth century did much to popularize monastic sites, whilst also bringing scholars to them in great numbers.

The growth of new towns in the middle years of the nineteenth century led in turn to a need for instant and respectable history. At Birkenhead, for instance, the ruins of the priory, long converted to a farm, suddenly assumed a new importance that resulted in their study and publication. They gave a past to a new industrial town and gave a new lease of life to buildings that were currently at risk. The same was true of the Cistercian abbey of Kirkstall on the banks of the River Aire to

the west of Leeds. When painted by Turner, Cotman, Girtin and Richardson, Kirkstall stood in open countryside (**colour plate 5**). As early as 1783 there were calls for the prevention of quarrying for building stone and the preservation of the ruins, work which was finally undertaken in 1799. In the early years of the nineteenth century the abbey ruins were opened to the public. In 1889, the site was finally acquired by the City of Leeds, and after archaeological study it was repaired and incorporated in a public park.

A new phase in the archaeological study of monastic sites began in the 1840s, starting with the work of Richard Walbran, who began his monumental excavation of Fountains Abbey in 1840, a project coupled with his extensive study of documents that was not completed until 1854. Walbran was first and foremost an historian, but his interest in Fountains was strictly archaeological. He was one of the first people actually to use the objects he found in his excavations to interpret the buildings he was studying and to reflesh the bare bones of a ruined site. Although he was frequently mistaken in his interpretation of particular buildings, mistaking for instance the ruins of the infirmary for those of the abbot's house and the warming-house for the kitchen, his published descriptions were full, with a wealth of detail that would be commendable in a modern study, and easily capable of reinterpretation. Many of his finds can still be identified. By the standard of his day, his method of excavation was unexceptionable, but the sharpness of his observations was remarkable. Whilst excavating in the choir area of the church,

the wheel of a cart that was passing over this part suddenly sank a foot or more deep in the earth and, on being raised, it was found that the slip had been occasioned by the fracture of a large earthenware vase that was buried immediately below the surface. As it had evidently been placed there at a remote period, the soil around was particularly examined, when it was discovered that, on the east side of the screen, and divided by the processional pathway, were two spaces of the form of a Roman letter L walled on the sides and flagged on the bottom. In that on the south side nothing was observed; but in the other, a large quantity of charcoal ashes; and to the astonishment of all who have seen them, nine vases or jugs of rude earthenware, each sufficiently capacious to have contained nearly two fluid gallons, fixed on their sides within the walls of the space, and also partially filled with charcoal. These ashes may have been cast here from the adjacent furnace, where the lead stripped from the house had evidently been melted into a marketable shape at the time of the dissolution; but why the vases should have been introduced is, so far as I can understand, on precedent, a case unique and unaccountable.

He had found the resonance pits below the late-medieval choir stalls, instantly recognizable from his description, and filled as he correctly supposed with the debris of spoliation. Walbran's recording of small and seemingly insignificant detail was a sign of the growing archaeological interest in monastic sites which was to increase throughout the second half of the

nineteenth century. He was an enthusiast, an amateur in the true sense of the word, taking his lead like John Martin before him from extant documents and not necessarily understanding what he found. His concern was to recover the plan of the buildings that did not survive above ground level and to examine the finer detail of those that did remain, and this he most certainly achieved.

Whilst Walbran was working amid the standing ruins at Fountains, a more remarkable excavation was being carried out at Lewes Priory, the senior Cluniac house in England. The coming of the railways to the Sussex coast in 1845–6 required the driving of a cutting 12.2 m (40 ft) wide and up to 3.6 m (12 ft) deep through the slightly-raised site of the thoroughly-demolished house. The heavy work of the navvies was supplemented by a group of local archaeologists led by A. M. Lower and J. L. Parsons, who recovered the plan and some architectural detail of the eastern end of the church and the greater part of the chapter-house. The excavators found clear evidence of the mines used by Thomas Cromwell's engineers to throw down the church. They also

6 *Stone-by-stone elevations of Fountains Abbey by J. A. Reeve, including these drawings of the church, remain the most accurate record of this important site.*

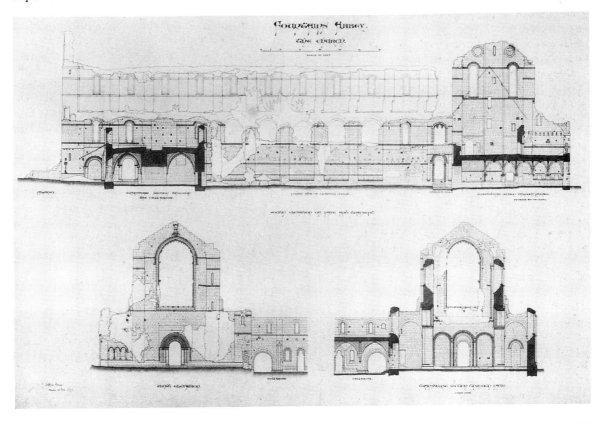

examined a large number of burials, recovering from the chapter-house lead caskets containing the bones of the founders, William de Warenne and Gundreda his wife, and the well-preserved body of a prior, with his habit, undergarments, shoes and red hair surviving. Further investigation of the site revealed in the railway cutting, included the monastic cemetery with more than 100 stone-lined graves being identified in addition to a great charnel pit aligned on the main axis of the church and only 2.4 m (8 ft) from its easternmost chapel, which the excavators chose to associate with the Battle of Lewes in 1264. It could just as easily have been connected with the late twelfth-century rebuilding of the church, which had been extended into the monastic cemetery. This rebuilding was also the probable context of the removal of the founders' remains from the choir to the chapter-house, and it was this rather than the recovery of lost buildings that most interested the excavators.

Monastic archaeology was to assume a more ordered form in the last quarter of the nineteenth century, the principles that were developed then having a lasting effect well into the twentieth century. Interest became more precisely architectural, with excavation used to answer specific questions. The architectural component was the detailed study of surviving fabric and the appreciation that it contained good evidence of the original form of buildings and their modification through time. The most remarkable manifestation of this can be seen in the stone-by-stone record of Fountains Abbey undertaken by J. A. Reeve at the suggestion of the architect William Burgess in the 1870s (6). It remains the most complete analysis of any abbey ruin and comprises an effective record of the buildings that were cleared of debris by Walbran a quarter of a century earlier. The most important aspect of this work was its publication as a permanent record of the largest monastic ruin in Britain.

The influence of Sir William St John Hope

The study of monasteries in the last three decades of the nineteenth century and the first decade of the twentieth century was dominated by one man, William St John Hope. He took his lead not from documents, but from the buildings themselves, seeking to establish ground plans from both standing masonry and buried foundations. He had a remarkable career, producing definitive analyses of every major class of monastery, surveying and excavating four Benedictine, two Cluniac, six Cistercian, four Augustinian, six Premonstratensian, one Templar and two Carthusian houses as well as one Augustinian nunnery and two houses of friars, towards the end of his career collaborating with two architects, John Bilson and Harold Brakspear. His method of working was basic. Describing the excavation of Alnwick Abbey specifically cleared for the Newcastle meeting of the Royal Archaeological Institute in 1884 on a site where only the

7 *Hope's excavation at Watton Priory was very much an exercise in following walls as this trench along the south wall of the canons' refectory shows. Although it was a quick method of recovering ground plans it did untold damage to archaeological deposits that post-dated the construction of individual walls.*

gatehouse remained extant, he said 'a more hopeless site for excavations could hardly be met with but trial trenches soon laid bare foundations of walls and by following these up in a scientific manner, the entire ground plan of the abbey was gradually disclosed'. This technique, if destructive of archaeological stratification, was used effectively at the Gilbertine house of Watton, one of the few Hope excavations for which a photographic record survives (**7**). The plan of Alnwick that Hope produced (**8**) was not phased to show periods of construction but it did show precisely what was found. Areas not excavated were labelled as such. What is remarkable about the excavation of Alnwick is the inclusion of the buildings of the Inner Court or service ranges. Previously, it was only the church, chapterhouse, and perhaps other cloister ranges, all buildings of some architectural sophistication, that had been studied. Hope was at a loss to interpret them for lack of parallels, describing them as 'a singular collection of chambers, ovens, fireplaces, etc., of which it is difficult to fix the precise age'. He was not even sure they were medieval.

In dealing with standing ruins, selective clearance was carried out to establish the outline of buildings, and small trenches, seldom

more than 0.3–0.6 m (1–2 ft) in width, were dug to examine key intersections. Where these have been re-excavated at Fountains Abbey and Mount Grace Priory, it is clear that they were placed with considerable skill and remarkable economy. They also indicate that the plans he produced required a great deal of intuitive guesswork and may not necessarily be as simple or as accurate as he assumed. A change can be recognized in his later work, with the production of coloured phase plans and more detailed descriptions of architectural detail, reflecting the influence and collaboration of Harold Brakspear at Beaulieu, Jervaulx and Fountains (where Brakspear drew the highly-detailed and analytical plans), and John Bilson at Kirkstall.

The value of Hope's work lay in the identification of individual buildings and the establishment of a series of 'standard' plans, and his bringing of academic respectability to monastic archaeology led to others following in his footsteps. His detailed studies of Fountains and Mount Grace remain classics even though both sites have been the scene of major recent excavations. Because he was led by standing buildings, his efforts (and those of his imitators) were concentrated on the church, cloister buildings and gatehouse, leading to a failure to understand that the monastic precinct contained many other buildings of architectural sophistication which could often be identified from documents.

8 *This plan of Alnwick Abbey, drawn by Hope in the 1880s, records every wall uncovered, providing a remarkably complete plan of the site though it does not attempt to show the date of the individual buildings.*

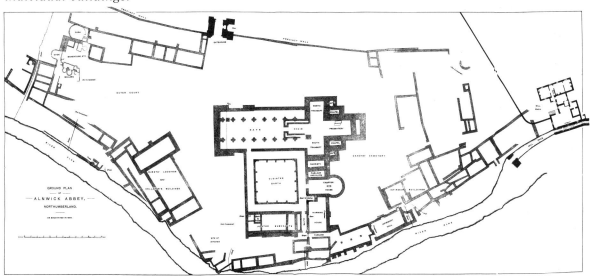

The widening concept of monastic archaeology

Harold Brakspear, whose archaeological career began with Hope in the 1890s, had a much wider concept of monastic archaeology than his mentor. He broke new ground in three respects: the study of the precinct as a whole; the recovery of buried buildings by area excavation as well as trenching; and the understanding that early buildings could be traced on the site of their successors. His first major excavation, taken over from Hope in 1899, was on an important Cistercian site, the abbey of Waverley, where his published report still stands the test of time. He worked from both surviving documents and the remaining ruins to identify the original church and cloister layout and its substantial rebuilding (**colour plate 3**). His excavation which was completed by 1900 did not simply look at the church, cloister and infirmary. He went on in 1901 to excavate substantially the laybrothers' infirmary and the Inner Court, an operation he completed the following year, together with a complicated brewhouse. In 1903, he excavated a further group of buildings to the north-west of the abbey church, badly disturbed by modern watercourses and difficult to identify, but probably the almonry. He then gave up, failing to find the inner gatehouse and gate chapel, known from John Aubrey's description of the 1660s, though not before he had carefully examined the 24 ha (60 acres) of the enclosed precinct, identifying evidence of water management.

His interest in the whole of the precinct recurred in his excavation and survey of Stanley Abbey in 1905–6, though he was not able to examine outlying buildings. He did, however, locate them on the ground and planned their apparent robber trenches along with the major earthworks of the precinct. Within the claustral nucleus he was able not only to identify the surviving walls and footings of the church

9 *Although the church at Bardney had been thoroughly demolished at the suppression, its floors and lower walls revealed before the First World War remained in excellent condition. The grave-slabs in the floor had been broken and depressed by the falling of masonry.*

and cloister buildings but also to trace walls which had been totally removed by excavating their robber trenches, indicating that he was aware of the latest developments in excavation technique. His plans included little in the way of supposition, a distinct improvement on the work of Hope, but his technique of excavation was more destructive of archaeological deposits, though he rarely excavated below the uppermost floors except in small trenches. Although he revealed the existence of an earlier church at Stanley Abbey on the same model as his primary church at Waverley, it was not followed up, and remains for future study.

The last great excavation of a monastic site before the First World War, was undertaken by the Rev. C. E. Laing at Bardney Abbey, a major Benedictine house on the fen edge in Lincolnshire. The method of excavation, trenching followed up by clearance to floor level, was very much that of Hope and Brakspear, but at Bardney it was taken to its logical conclusion: the wholesale exposure of structures, and in particular the church (9). Work was stopped by the war and by Laing's death, and several peripheral areas still remain to be excavated. Only the central buildings and the gatehouses had been examined, and they were left exposed to public view within a wall built from fallen stone. Laing had unintentionally demonstrated the future for monastic ruins in the twentieth century. Unfortunately, the low walls were never conserved and began to fall apart, being reburied in the 1930s to protect them from the weather.

Monastic archaeology and the state

The Ancient Monuments Act of 1911 permitted the government to take into state guardianship any ruins or buildings of archaeological and architectural importance, and allowed for their repair and display to the public. The effect that this was to have on monastic studies was dramatic. Many of the most important abbey and priory remains were taken into the guardianship of the Office of Works and its successors, with the express intention of repairing and conserving their fabric for the first time. Because the emphasis was on conservation and display, however, it tended to be only the church and claustral ranges that were taken, divorcing the central group of buildings from the normally less well-preserved areas of the inner and outer courts and even placing these

areas at risk. Many of the earliest guardianships were in the north of England, where the survival of fabric was greatest, and included several sites that had not been available to Hope or his contemporaries. Among many other sites, Rievaulx, a completely untouched site (10) was taken in 1918, Roche in 1921, Byland, again barely disturbed, in 1922, Furness and Titchfield in 1923, Egglestone in 1925, Monk Bretton in 1932, St Augustine's, Canterbury, in 1939, Shap in 1948, Creake and Lilleshall in 1950, Thornton in 1954, and Fountains in 1966. Central to the early policy of state care was the Chief Inspector of Ancient Monuments, Sir Charles Peers. His own monastic interests can be seen in an active policy of acquisition and in the series of site guides he produced, and his policies were to have a lasting effect on monastic studies well into the 1960s.

Peers was not simply content to conserve the upstanding ruins, which he did with an exemplary respect for what he found, adding new masonry only where it was needed to support historic fabric, he also undertook the excavation of the sites to recover their full plans, recovering the remains of demolished walls and internal fittings. By modern standards, his excavations were brutal but effective, involving the clearance of all fallen debris, including the evidence for the latest occupation and demolition, but stopping at the latest floor levels. His approach developed those of Hope and Brakspear, but the resources he had at his command meant that, like Laing at Bardney, he could strip large areas and, with state funding, could conserve what he found for posterity. It is Peers who was responsible for the didactic display of vegetation-free masonry and closely-mown lawns that are still associated with monastic ruins.

Rievaulx Abbey, one of the first sites to be tackled by Peers in 1919, remains today very much as Peers left it (11), stripped of its latest occupation and demolition levels by a small army of workmen, many of whom were unemployed veterans of the First World War. There was little archaeological supervision of any kind, the day-to-day decisions being taken by the site foreman, who was a stone mason. In spite of this, rudimentary records were made of the most significant finds, and most, if not all, of the fallen architectural detail, coins, small-finds, and even pottery can still be identified to a findspot. No attempt was made to

10 *Rievaulx Abbey was one of the few abbey sites that had not been dug into the nineteenth century, many of its buildings including the nave of the church were totally buried.*

excavate below the latest surviving floors, with the result that most of the structural archaeology that will identify phases of construction or even earlier phases of building is still intact. The loss of post-monastic deposits, which would include perhaps the evidence for the reuse of buildings after the suppression, was not considered important at the time and, though it had interested Brakspear, was thought to be a necessary price to pay for the large-scale recovery of important claustral plans. The simplistic idea that only monastic remains were significant on monastic sites was to continue into the 1950s, with the loss of many important post-medieval buildings, such as the seventeenth-century farmhouse built into the gate-

house at Monk Bretton Priory, as Inspectors trained by Peers pursued his purist approach.

Few records survive to show how Peers and his workforce went about their task of clearing monastic sites, and photographs of work in progress are rare in the extreme. Some survive for Whitby Abbey (**12**) showing the scale of the work undertaken. Up to 2.7 m (9 ft) of fallen masonry had to be removed to recover the plan of the church (see Chapter 6). The fallen debris was not simply rubble discarded by stone robbers but great sections of superstructure such as the western tower arch and three bays of the clerestory of the nave, which had fallen intact as the ruin decayed. The photographs clearly show the light railway used to clear away the debris, to be dumped on unexcavated parts of the site where it obscured other buried buildings. Whitby was a site with an intriguing early history and one of the few sites that Peers actually excavated below its latest floors. First, the remains of an earlier Norman church were

11 *In 1921, the church at Rievaulx looked very different. Up to 3m (9ft) of fallen debris had been removed to expose one of the earliest known Cistercian naves in Europe, seen here shortly after its conservation by the Office of Works.*

excavated (see **22**), and in 1924, following the discovery of Saxon buildings below the outer parlour on the south side of the church, the large-scale excavation of buried structures belonging to the Saxon monastery was undertaken first to the west of the nave and then on the north side of the church (see **34**). As with general clearance, there was a lack of constant archaeological supervision resulting in a poor quality of record, leaving the pre-conquest monastery both damaged and imperfectly understood.

The work done by the Office of Works and excavations at non-guardianship sites, such as Glastonbury, Whalley and Sempringham, set a new standard for monastic archaeology and brought it firmly to the public's attention. Sites once conserved were opened to the public and proved immediately popular. Peers and his successors wrote a series of academically sound and remarkably informative guides to individual sites, all of which featured an accurate and phased ground plan, and which summarized the sites' history and architectural development. They also published more detailed considerations of their work in the academic press, and both these media were to have a lasting effect, bringing scholarship to the general public and with it an appreciation of the monuments. Whilst the study of monastic sites in the nineteenth century had been a matter for interested individuals, the twentieth century saw its exploitation for the masses. From those

12 *Whitby Abbey, a hitherto untouched site, was cleared of fallen debris in the early 1920s, revealing large parts of the fallen superstructure including this part of the western arch below the central tower which fell in 1830.*

masses came the next generation of monastic scholars, who were to bring analytical excavation, detailed documentary research and a new appreciation of the potential of our monastic resources.

From the early nineteenth century, research on monastic sites had been driven by an obsession with the recovery of ground plans to the exclusion of the many other aspects of religious life that the sites could evidence. Perhaps the turning point was marked in the early 1950s, first by the aerial study of monastic sites which reawakened interest in non-claustral buildings and sites not in state care, and then by a growing interest in medieval archaeology which had previously been seen simply as a tool of the historian. Sites without standing masonry, so far largely ignored, were coming under threat from more intensive agriculture and from housing or office development. Starting with the excavation of the London Charterhouse and part of the church of Bermondsey Abbey by W. F. Grimes, the active study of monastic sites passed from those who were primarily motivated by architectural history to those who were primarily archaeologists interested in recording all aspects of the site they excavated. The result has been that in the last 40 years far more has been learned about the origins, growth, and demise of abbeys and priories in England, and a much fuller picture can be reconstructed of sites examined previously. Much work was government sponsored,

13 *The total excavation of Grove Priory between 1973 and 1989 has shown the complications of a multi-phase site which was truly monastic only for a relatively short period between 1164 and 1300 (Evelyn Baker).*

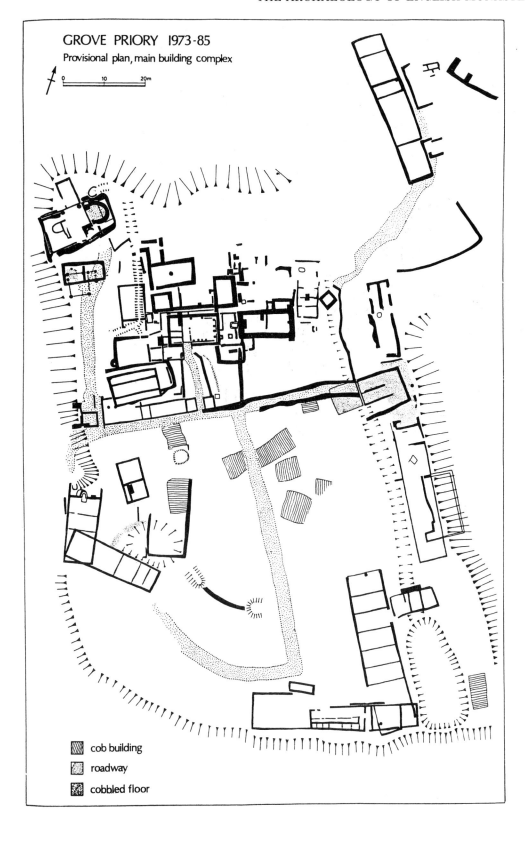

GROVE PRIORY 1973-85

Provisional plan, main building complex

0   10   20m

cob building

roadway

cobbled floor

initially on sites threatened with destruction: the Trinitarian house of Thelsford, the Gilbertine houses of Haverholme and North Ormsby, the Cluniac priory at Faversham, the nunneries of Elstow and Sopwell, and the Templar preceptory of South Witham. Privately sponsored work ran in parallel with rescue archaeology, with major work undertaken by Leeds Museum at Kirkstall Abbey and by H. H. Swinnerton at Lenton Priory. The results of these excavations inevitably led to a change in the way sites in the care of the state were treated. No longer were sites simply cleared of debris. Now they were properly excavated, leading to a fuller understanding of their potential. The pioneering work of Roy Gilyard-Beer at Gisborough Priory and Muchelney Abbey and Andrew Saunders at St Augustine's Abbey, Canterbury, was followed in the late 1960s by large-scale excavations at Mount Grace Priory and Rosemary Cramp's analyses of the Saxon and later monastery at Jarrow, and more recently those at Bayham, Battle, Fountains, Gloucester Blackfriars, Rievaulx and Southwick.

New directions in monastic archaeology

From the 1970s there has been an increasing interest in monastic archaeology and a further change in the direction of research, with a growing emphasis on the economic aspects of religious life. Major excavations have taken place at Norton Priory, Bradwall Abbey and Sandwell Priory and continues at Bordesley Abbey, providing, as did Birkenhead Priory and Kirkstall Abbey in the nineteenth century, a focus for new towns. Redevelopment on urban sites has led to the large-scale excavation of friary sites, most notably in Guildford, Leicester, Newcastle and Beverley, and other houses such as that of the Gilbertines at York. The difference is that the recent excavations have examined the sites involved totally, looking particularly at the way sites grew and were managed, using not only the buildings but also their cultural contents and the burials they contained. At Bordesley, for instance, not only are the cloister buildings involved, but the whole of the precinct has also been studied, with selective excavation of buildings in it – to date, the gate chapel and an industrial mill. At Norton, the tile kiln that provided much of the flooring for the church has been examined, and much of the precinct is preserved within a public park. In the field of rescue archaeology,

three sites have made an important contribution to the study of the economic basis of monastic life: Grove Priory (**13**), where the whole site has been examined in detail; Waltham Abbey (**84**), where large areas of the outer court and home grange have been excavated; and Thornholme Priory (**14**), where excavation has defined the development of the service areas over four centuries. Additionally, recent work in the outer court at Fountains Abbey has begun the study of the economy of the richest Cistercian monastery in England with the analysis of two buildings central to its management – the mill (**76**) and the wool-house (**77**) – coupled with a re-examination of the church and cloister buildings that has substantially altered their accepted interpretation. The scale of research has been substantial, with some excavation being carried out on nearly 200 sites since 1945, almost one-fifth of those available.

Since John Martin persuaded the gardener to clear out the chapter-house at Fountains Abbey in 1790, monastic archaeology has come of age and permitted an accurate impression of monastic life to be recreated. There are still many gaps in our knowledge, and every new excavation will add to our understanding. Monasteries are no longer simply churches and cloister buildings, no longer enclosed precincts with many other buildings, they are at last seen for what they were: major economic corporations whose actions affected all of medieval England. They were of course much more than this, and in our attempts to understand their function we have tended to lose sight of their purpose, and very reason for being. They should be seen not simply as objects of curiosity, but seen as they were by their builders, as self-sustaining oratories to God and workshops of prayer. Archaeology can provide the how, but it cannot provide the why.

14 *Thornholme Priory, an earthwork site with no surviving ruins, is a good example of a total precinct, with the cloister buildings occupying the higher ground (to the right of the ruined farm buildings) but the rest of the precinct made up of enclosed courts with many buildings. Large parts of the service areas of the house were excavated from 1974 to 1980 (Cambridge University Coll.)*

2

The monastic church

The church was the largest and most important building of the monastery. Used for a continuing round of services, its scale, quality, and fittings reflected the importance of the community and its patrons. A number of monastic churches survive, amongst the greatest being the cathedrals of Durham, Gloucester, Peterborough, Canterbury, Winchester, Carlisle, Worcester and Chester. Others survive as parish churches, like Selby, Christchurch, Dorchester or Pershore. Many more survive as fragments where they had been partially used as parish churches in the Middle Ages, at Boxgrove, Bridlington, Crowland, Malmesbury, Leominster, Malvern, Bolton or Binham. Others survive in varying states of preservation as roofless ruins, like Fountains or Glastonbury, Kirkham or Netley, Bury St Edmunds or Rievaulx. Few churches remain exactly as they were first built, and none retains all its original furnishings and decoration. It is only by the comparison of surviving examples and the excavation of earlier buildings that the development of monastic churches can be recovered.

Reduced to its basic provisions, the convent church was a house for the altar, the choir where mass and the seven offices or services were sung, additional altars for the religious who were priests and required to say a personal mass, and for the burial of the founder and his family. Additionally, a part of the church might be reserved for the laity. Whilst changing liturgy, increasing wealth, and growing communities might have led to changes in the planning of monastic churches, the need to provide for these facilities remained constant and can be seen in the earliest buildings known.

The churches of Saxon monasteries

The first churches are known only from excavation, and the recovery of the plan of the church, founded in 598 by St Augustine for his mission to Kent outside the walls of late Roman Canterbury, between 1900 and 1931 began the study of the earliest monastic churches in England. Dedicated to St Peter and St Paul, St Augustine's church was dedicated, and thus most probably completed, in 613. All that remained below the great cruciform church of St Augustine's Abbey that succeeded it in the late eleventh century were the lower courses of walls built from reused Roman brick set in mortar. It was a simple rectangular building with a porch at its west end and porticus or chapels ranged on both its north and its south sides (15). Its east end had been destroyed by later building but, if it conformed to other early churches in Kent, it would have terminated in an apse, rounded inside but polygonal externally. The nave and porch of the church were floored with mortar containing a high proportion of crushed brick and chalk, very much like Roman *opus signinum*. The eastern porticus were used for burials. That on the north side dedicated to St Gregory is known to have been used for the burial of the first six archbishops, and the tile-built tombs of Justus,

15 *The church of St Peter, St Paul and St Augustine and the church of St Mary at Canterbury with associated cloister buildings of the tenth and eleventh centuries that lie below the Norman church and cloister of St Augustine's Abbey.*

Late 6th and early 7th century

Ditto destroyed by later building

Probably 10th century

Ditto inferred

Mid 11th century

Uncertain

SITES OF TOMBS

A Justus
B Mellitus
C Laurence
D Honorius
E Deusdedit
F Augustine
G Berhtwald
H Theodore
J Luithard
K Queen Bertha
L King Ethelbert

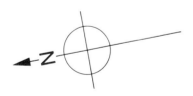

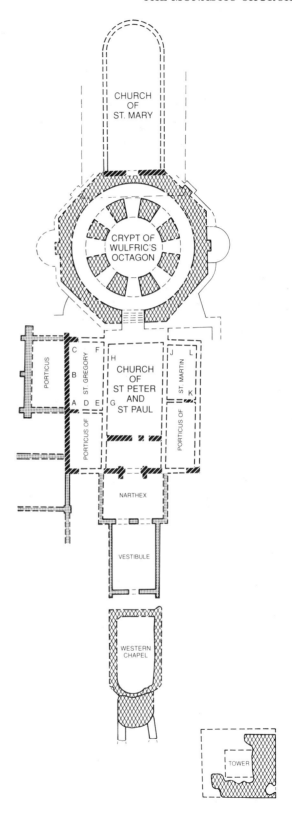

CHURCH OF ST. MARY

CRYPT OF WULFRIC'S OCTAGON

PORTICUS

PORTICUS OF ST GREGORY

CHURCH OF ST PETER AND ST PAUL

PORTICUS OF ST. MARTIN

NARTHEX

VESTIBULE

WESTERN CHAPEL

TOWER

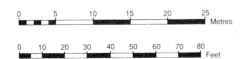

Mellitus and Laurentius survive against the north wall very much in the state they were left in 1090 when the bodies were translated to the new Norman church. In the south porticus of St Martin, the royal patrons Ethelbert of Kent and his queen were buried. In 620, a second church dedicated to St Mary was built to the east on the same axis as the first church, to be followed by a third church, that of St Pancras, further east still. St Mary's church was destroyed but for the footings of its west wall when the crypt below the eastern arm of the Norman church was built between 1070 and 1087, though there are substantial remains of St Pancras, reused as the cemetery church of the Norman monastery. The building of a series of small churches in line was a peculiar aspect of Saxon monasteries, and similar arrangements to those at Canterbury have been noted at Glastonbury, Winchester, Jarrow and Monkwearmouth.

16 *The earliest Anglo-Saxon churches at Canterbury were more substantial than their plans might suggest, and are shown here reconstructed by Richard Gem.*

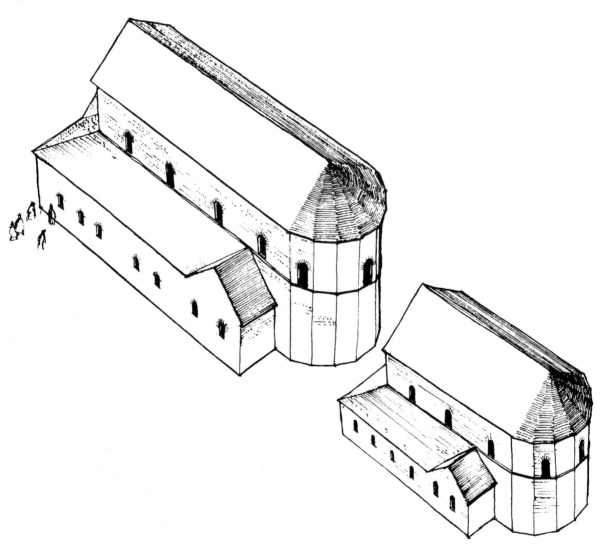

The importance of the Canterbury churches is that they were observed to develop, and that progress was elucidated by excavation and historical research. From the surviving excavated remains and by analogy with other Saxon buildings it is possible to attempt a reconstruction of their original appearance (16). Gradually they grew together to form a composite church much more like the great monastic churches found in continental Europe. Lack of burial space in the porticus of St Gregory led to the building of a new chapel to the north, this time not of Roman brick but of rag-stone and flint and dating between 731 and 792. This work pre-dated a major extension of the church of St Peter and St Paul undertaken by St Dunstan and completed in 978, when the church was rededicated to St Peter, St Paul and St Augustine. The context for major rebuilding was the general European monastic reform movement of the tenth century that occasioned the *Regularis Concordia*, a code of practice drawn up by the Council of Winchester in 973. Specifically the *Regularis Concordia* defined three liturgical areas within the church, each with its own altar: at the west end (*oratorium*), in the nave (*ecclesia*), and at the east end of the church (*chorus*). At Canterbury this was marked by the westward extension of the nave into the old porch, the construction of a new porch or narthex to the west, and a vestibule beyond that. Further west, a chapel with a western apse was provided. Two-storey transepts were provided over the eastern porticus, and it is likely that the nave was raised in height to match these. The upper stories of the transepts acted as galleries above the nave altar, which was itself backed by an inserted

17 *The growth of the Canterbury churches, first under St Dunstan and later under Abbot Wulfric, was dramatic as can be seen from Dr Gem's second reconstruction.*

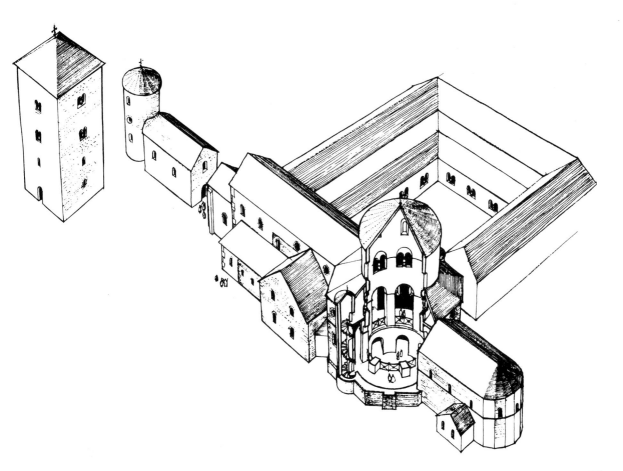

cross-wall that divided the area of the *ecclesia* from the eastern *chorus*.

The final stage of development of this church came after 1047 when Abbot Wulfric joined the church of St Peter, St Paul and St Augustine with that of St Mary, using a great rotunda based on that of St Benigne at Dijon (**17**), a project left incomplete in about 1073 when Abbot Scotland began his rebuilding of the whole church to a Norman plan. It was Wulfric who also added towers to the west of his extended church.

Similar development can be seen in the abbey church of Glastonbury (**18**) where a monastic community had existed from perhaps as early as the sixth century. The earliest church, the

vetusta ecclesia, was timber-built and of uncertain but great age. Its site is now marked by the crypt of the surviving lady chapel. To its east, King Ine built a rectangular stone church at the turn of the eighth century, with flanking porticus and an eastern chancel of square plan set over a mausoleum. It was linked to the original wooden church by a walled yard. This building, located by excavation, was modified

18 *Excavation below the medieval church at Glastonbury has revealed the fragmentary remains of the Saxon monastery church built by King Ine in about 700 and later extended by St Dunstan (after Fernie).*

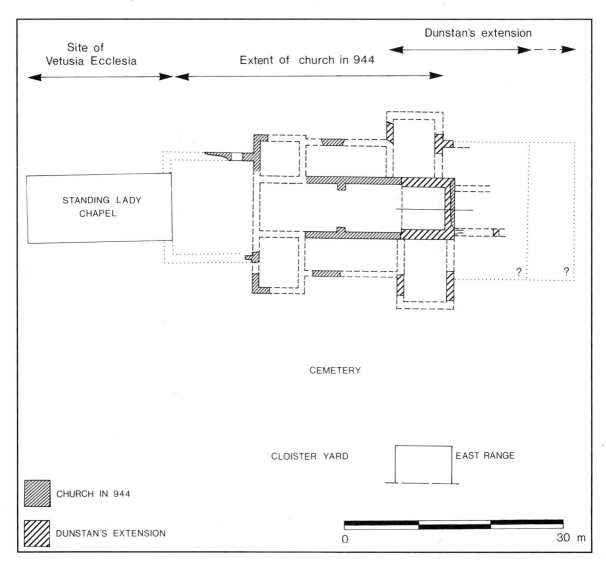

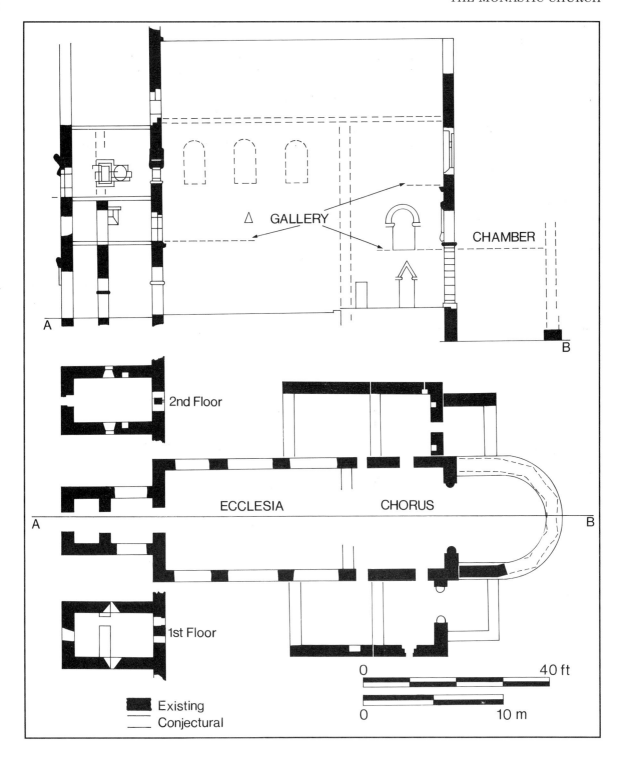

19 *Deerhurst, the best-preserved Saxon monastic church in England, survives substantially as built. Its recent study allows its late Saxon form to be recovered in remarkable detail (after Taylor and Taylor).*

substantially by St Dunstan, abbot from 944 to 956. His biographer William of Malmesbury records that he 'added a tower to this church, considerably lengthened it and, so that it might form a square in length and breadth, he added aisles or porticus as they call them'. Ine's mausoleum was destroyed to build the tower, with its walls refaced and widened to carry the superstructure. To the north and south of the tower, slightly irregular porticus were added in the form of transepts, much in the manner of the later work at Canterbury, and from a later documentary source it is clear that these were two-storeyed, with galleries looking down onto the nave altar. To the east, Dunstan built his new chancel with flanking porticus to north and south. The eastern termination has not been traced by excavation.

In both these cases, an excavated ground-plan has given a clear impression of the extent and development of each building, though it can tell very little about the long-demolished elevation. Documentary sources imply churches of more than one storey, and this is confirmed by surviving churches from as early as the seventh century. The finest example of a surviving Saxon monastery church is that of Deerhurst (19), built by 804 and ceasing to be an abbey before the Norman conquest. The archaeological study of its surviving fabric coupled with the excavation of demolished elements has revealed it to be a complicated structure. The first phase of building, overlaying an earlier Christian cemetery, comprised a rectangular building with a porch at its west end and no separate chancel, its walls surviving in places to a full height of only 3.6 m (12 ft). At some point before the mid tenth century an apsidal chancel was added. Although it was built from a level almost 1.5 m (5 ft) below the floor of the nave, excavation proved that it did not contain a crypt or mausoleum. The church was extensively rebuilt in the tenth century, perhaps as a result of the reform of the monastery by St Oswald about 970. The nave was raised to its present height of 12.2 m (40 ft) and a square presbytery or choir defined at its east end by the insertion of a cross-wall. The apsidal chancel was rebuilt in polygonal form, its outer face decorated with stripwork at the angles. High up on the surviving south wall above a string-course was a pediment outlined with stripwork and containing the fine carving of an angel. Two-storey porticus were built to the

north and south of the choir, with wide, round-headed openings at the first floor perhaps leading to galleries. Excavation showed that additional porticus were added, first to the west and then to the east, overlapping the construction of the new chancel. They too appear to have had an upper floor. An upper chamber in the chancel is evidenced by a wide opening in the east wall of the choir with a pair of corbels below it to support a gallery. Similarly, the original porch at the west end of the nave was raised to form a tower, perhaps in two stages. At first-floor level an oratory was created, its door set off-centre to respect the position of the altar and leading to a narrow gallery at the west end of the nave. Above were two further chambers, that at second floor level having a door in its west wall leading to an external gallery and a pair of triangular-headed windows looking down into the nave.

The churches of Norman monasteries

The traumatic conquest of England in 1066 sounded the death knell of Saxon monasticism and the introduction of new architectural models from Normandy that had developed from far-reaching reforms of the continental church. In England, this change had effectively begun a decade before the Norman invasion, with Edward the Confessor's rebuilding of the abbey church at Westminster. Limited excavation below the floor of its thirteenth-century successor has revealed sufficient low walling and foundation-work to show that King Edward's church was closely modelled on the abbey church of Jumièges, begun around 1040. At Westminster this is evidenced by a long aisled nave with paired western towers, a crossing with fully developed transepts and an eastern arm that terminated in an apse. The introduction of Norman abbots into English houses, and the founding of many new monasteries, some albeit on old sites, led to a dramatic change in church planning to accord with current European liturgy that is well represented in the archaeological record.

The new liturgy was to dictate the form of monastic churches up to the second quarter of the sixteenth century and can still be identified in its simplest form in the surveys of convent buildings made in 1535 prior to the suppression of the English monasteries. At Wilberfoss Priory, a poor Benedictine nunnery in the Vale of York, the nave of the church was used by the parish and survives. The nuns' church was described thus: 'The churche conteynith in length lx ffoote and in bradith xxij ffoote w[t]yn, and seylid aboue w[t] goode substancyalle bourdes, and coueryd w[t] slates, hauynge xvj goode stalles in the quere for nonnes, and the high alter w[t] a fayer new ffronte alle gilted which conteynith by estimacon x*li*, ij alters in the quere and one benethe, ix glasse wyndowes containing by estimacon lxx foote of glasse.' Although the nuns of Wilberfoss had a rectangular church (**20**), its layout was similar to that of the cruciform church adopted by most monasteries. The choir, which formed the centre of the ritual layout, normally lay beneath the crossing or at the east end of the nave, with the principal altar lying to its east in the presbytery. Two altars were normally placed against the pulpitum screen that enclosed the choir at its west end, serving a space of one or two bays called the retrochoir. To the west

of the retrochoir a second screen, the rood screen, closed off the monastic part of the church, and against the west face of this was placed the nave altar. Further altars were provided for the use of the religious who were priests and required to say personal masses, either in the transepts or against the east wall of the church behind the high altar.

The rebuilding of St Augustine's monastery

20 *Redrawn from the surviving remains of the parochial nave and from a detailed survey of the house made in 1535, the plan of the small Benedictine nunnery of Wilberfoss serves to demonstrate a fairly typical monastic layout. The church, a simple rectangular building, was divided into two parts, the parish church and the nuns' choir.*

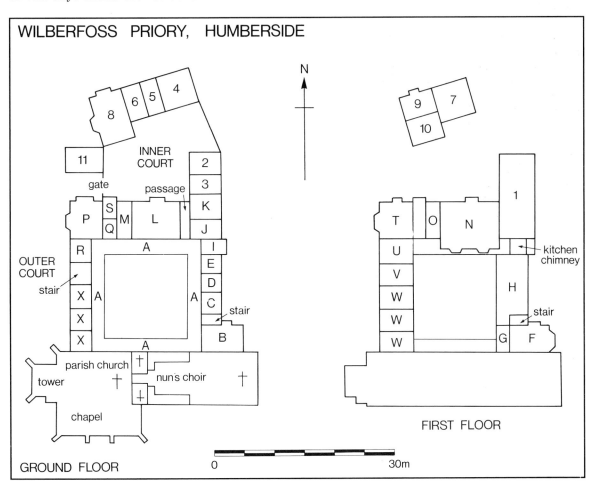

WILBERFOSS PRIORY, HUMBERSIDE

N

GROUND FLOOR

0   30m

FIRST FLOOR

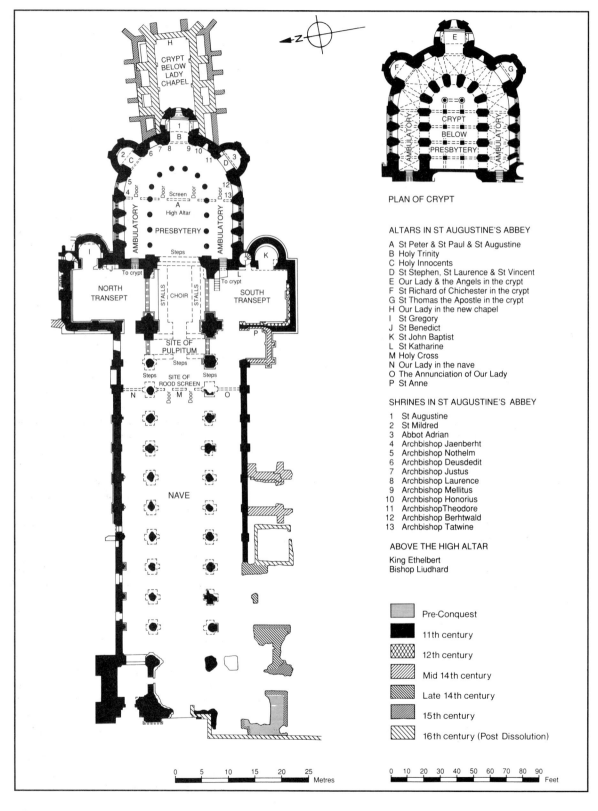

PLAN OF CRYPT

ALTARS IN ST AUGUSTINE'S ABBEY

A St Peter & St Paul & St Augustine
B Holy Trinity
C Holy Innocents
D St Stephen, St Laurence & St Vincent
E Our Lady & the Angels in the crypt
F St Richard of Chichester in the crypt
G St Thomas the Apostle in the crypt
H Our Lady in the new chapel
I St Gregory
J St Benedict
K St John Baptist
L St Katharine
M Holy Cross
N Our Lady in the nave
O The Annunciation of Our Lady
P St Anne

SHRINES IN ST AUGUSTINE'S ABBEY

1   St Augustine
2   St Mildred
3   Abbot Adrian
4   Archbishop Jaenberht
5   Archbishop Nothelm
6   Archbishop Deusdedit
7   Archbishop Justus
8   Archbishop Laurence
9   Archbishop Mellitus
10 Archbishop Honorius
11 Archbishop Theodore
12 Archbishop Berhtwald
13 Archbishop Tatwine

ABOVE THE HIGH ALTAR

King Ethelbert
Bishop Liudhard

Pre-Conquest

11th century

12th century

Mid 14th century

Late 14th century

15th century

16th century (Post Dissolution)

0   5   10   15   20   25
Metres

0 10 20 30 40 50 60 70 80 90
Feet

21 *The plan of the Norman and later church at St Augustine's Abbey, Canterbury, recovered by excavation since the late nineteenth century, clearly shows the form of the new 'pilgrimage' churches introduced from the Continent. The multiplicity of altars and shrines, located from medieval sources, amplifies the importance of the building.*

at Canterbury is well documented and attested by excavation, and shows the typical process involved in the building of a great church which was often built in identifiable stages (**21**). Abbot Scotland began the building of a great cruciform pilgrimage church in or after 1070 to house the relics contained by the old monastic churches, building an apsidal presbytery over a crypt. At his death, only the presbytery, transepts, crossing, and first two bays of the nave had been completed, and from Goscelin's contemporary narrative, the convent was deeply divided over the necessary decision to demolish the greater part of the ancient church of St Peter, St Paul and St Augustine and disturb the burials it contained. The new nave had been laid out, but only its foundations were completed. Scotland's death in 1087 left the decision to his successor, Wido, who completed the crossing tower and transferred the relics from the old church to the new in 1090. Wido continued with the construction of the nave and completed the demolition of the old church. Though he changed the design of his predecessor's intended nave, adding additional foundation work for a pair of western towers, the two phases of construction could only be identified by excavation. He was not to see the western towers built, however, for he died in 1099. The architectural detail of the north-west tower (see **2**), which survived until 1822, shows it to be the work of his successor Hugh de Fleury. The architectural fragments which survived the wholesale destruction of the church in the middle years of the sixteenth century show it to have been a building of the highest and most developed quality. The abbey church of St Augustine was not unique but one of a series of monumental Norman churches designed to change the architecture of the English church. A closely comparable church was built at Bury St Edmunds to house the shrine of the King martyr St Edmund between about 1090 and 1142. Its model was very clearly St Augustine's at Canterbury.

The majority of churches belonging to the first half century after the conquest however were neither as large nor as elaborate as those built to house shrines. At Whitby Abbey, for instance, a new Norman house was established amidst the ruins of St Hild's monastery in 1078. Because of a dispute with the founder, William de Percy, the site was temporarily abandoned, and building is unlikely to have started for perhaps a decade or more. The foundations of the east end and transepts of this late-eleventh-century church were recovered by Sir Charles Peers in 1924–5 (**22**). Although the remains were fragmentary, lying as they do below a rebuilding of the early thirteenth century, enough remains to reconstruct the original plan. The presbytery was aisled and of two bays, whilst to the east was a sanctuary of two more bays marked by shallow pilaster buttresses and terminating in an apse. The aisles themselves also ended in apses. Transepts of a single bay were traced below their Early English successors, with a single apsidal chapel opening eastwards from each. More survived of these chapels than any other part of the structure, being buried below the raised floors of the thirteenth-century transept chapels. Up to two courses of fine ashlar casing survived, with paired pilaster buttresses on the outer face. The southern chapel was somewhat larger than that on the north, a feature confirmed by small-scale re-excavation in 1987, which allowed for the correction of minor errors in Peers' plan. Although the plan of the late-eleventh-century nave was not recovered, nor apparently sought, it is likely to have been almost as long as its fourteenth-century replacement, for Peers located the mid-twelfth-century outer parlour at the north end of the west cloister range, proving the western extent of the cloister. The position of the outer parlour would also indicate that the nave was aisled like the presbytery. The value of the Norman plan at Whitby is that it demonstrates the layout of a middle-rank monastic church of the first generation after the conquest. An indication of its lost elevations can be gained from an unfinished church at Lastingham, built between 1078 and 1086, by a group of Whitby monks who moved on to establish the great Benedictine abbey at York in that year. At Lastingham, the presbytery, crossing and first bay of the nave survive, a closely comparable structure to the excavated church at Whitby,

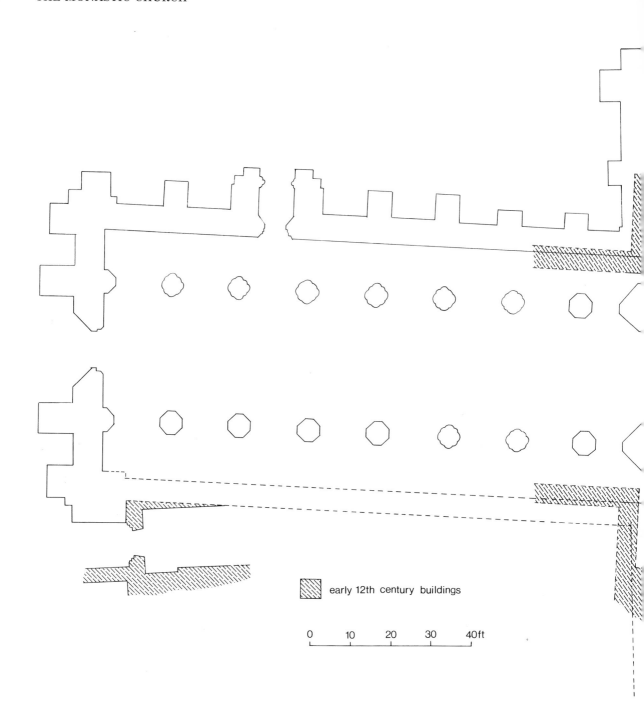

22 *The abbey church at Whitby is a building of the thirteenth and fourteenth centuries overlaying the foundations of a church of late eleventh and twelfth century date. Excavation in 1924–5 recovered a substantial part of its plan.*

early 12th century buildings

0   10   20   30   40ft

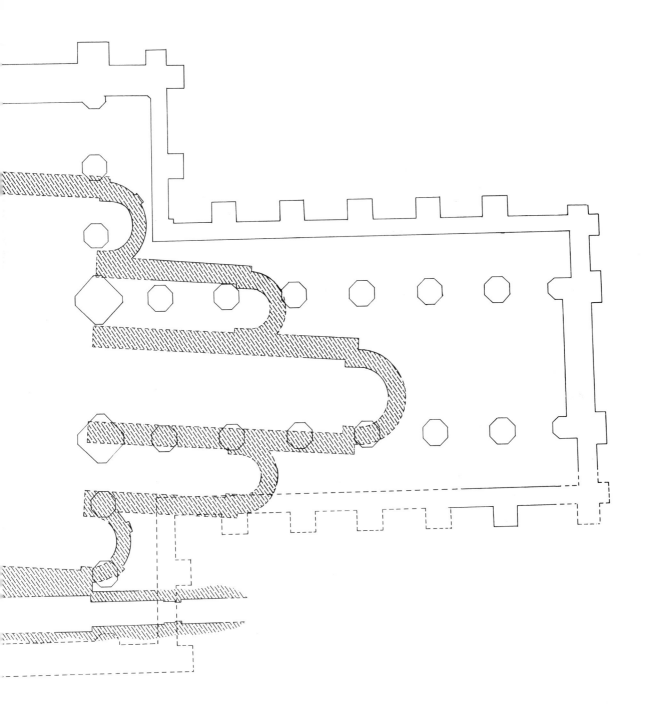

23 *Built by monks from Whitby, but left unfinished in 1086, the parish church of Lastingham
retains one bay of its nave, its crossing, transept
and presbytery, a building close in date to the
Norman church at Whitby which must have
looked very much like it.*

which must be its near contemporary (**23**).

The 'standard' Benedictine plan introduced
with the Norman reform of liturgy was not to
last unaltered by religious reforms that were
sweeping Europe from the late eleventh century
and that led to wide variations in church
planning. The Cistercians simplified their
churches and favoured substantial aisled naves
that housed the choir of their laybrothers,
whilst the canons generally preferred unaisled
naves and long presbyteries to house their main
altars. The Knights Templar built their naves
on a circular plan, basing the design on the
Church of the Holy Sepulchre at Jerusalem.
Their principal house in England, the London
Temple, survives; it was consecrated in 1185, a
larger version of the preceptory churches
spread across the country. That at Temple

Bruer in Lincolnshire was first excavated in
1833, one of the earliest monastic churches to
be so examined. Further work by Hope in 1907
has refined the plan (**24**). As originally built in
the 1160s, the circular nave was supported on
an arcade of eight cylindrical piers and was
surrounded by an aisle with rib-vaults. It was
entered on its west side by a porch that enclosed
a flight of steps, indicating a raised floor in the
nave itself. To the east was a short apsidal
presbytery built over a crypt which was reached
from the nave aisle by stepped passages.
Towards the end of the twelfth century the
eastern arm was extended with a square termination. To this new presbytery were added two
squat towers, the southern of which still survives. On the suppression of the Templars in
1308–12, the site was granted to the Knights
Hospitlar who favoured churches of similar
form. The Hospitlars added an aisle to the south
of the choir but otherwise barely altered this
remarkable little church.

24 *The circular church of the Knights Templar
at Temple Bruer as excavated by Hope in 1907.*

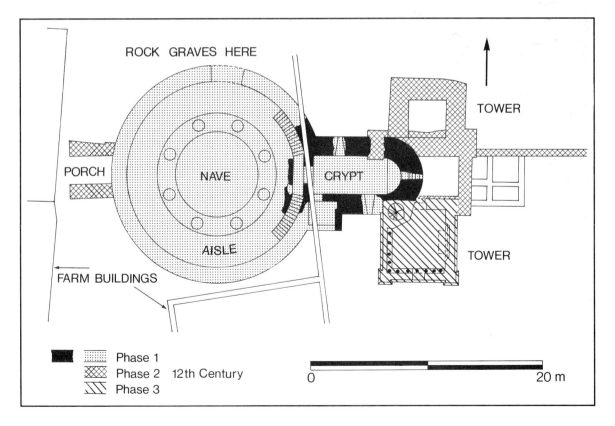

The development of monastic churches

Monastic churches tended to be rebuilt as a house's economy expanded and as liturgy developed, and few remained as originally built by the sixteenth century. Thus the scholar is faced with having to untangle masonry of several periods in one building. Alterations might be simple, modernizing an old church by replacing its windows with more up-to-date designs. Frequently more drastic measures were taken, with extensive or wholesale rebuilding. Three examples of rebuilt or remodelled churches that have had the added benefit of excavation to recover the plan of demolished elements demonstrate the methods employed to extend and modify the building throughout the life of the house.

The first is the Cistercian monastery of Fountains, where excavation in 1980 (**25**) revealed that the present church is the third to stand on that site. The monks who established Fountains late in 1132 were Benedictines from York who wished to join the Cistercian order. Their actions are known from a contemporary chronicle graphically proved by excavation. In 1133 they sought advice from Abbot Bernard of Clairvaux who sent an experienced monk, Geoffroi d'Ainai, to instruct them in Cistercian liturgy and to oversee the construction of a temporary timber monastery. In 1135 a building fund was established, and a small stone church was begun. This church was damaged in a disastrous fire in 1146, was repaired, and subsequently replaced by a more suitable and elaborate building, which was certainly under construction in 1154.

The excavation within the south transept of the standing church, which had previously been considered to be the church of 1135, revealed first the remains of two substantial timber buildings. The first was aligned east-west, with double post-pits marking doors in its north and south walls, and was the oratory or church. The second, lying north-south, on the south side of the oratory, was a domestic building, its deep post-pits suggesting that it was of two storeys. Contemporary accounts of other Cistercian monasteries would suggest that this was the refectory at ground level with a dormitory above.

Cutting through these two buildings were the foundations of a fire-damaged stone building, the south transept of a cruciform church with two eastern chapels. The altars in these chapels survived, their positions showing that the inner chapel extended further to the east than that to the south. In the north-east corner of the excavated area, the step up into the short presbytery survived, together with traces of a mortar floor. In the crossing area of this church a small area of original flooring survived, a skimming of mortar sealed below a deposit of rushes that had floored the choir area. The position of the choir stalls themselves was provided by a screen wall that cut the transept off from the crossing. This screen wall must have had only a small door in its east end for,

25 *Excavation of the south transept at Fountains Abbey in 1980 revealed the foundation of a smaller and earlier church that had been burned. Below that were the post-pits of the earliest buildings of the monastery, a temporary timber church aligned east-west, the double post-pits marking its doors, and a north-south domestic building whose post-pits run parallel to the west wall of the transept.*

as the chronicle hinted, the main body of the church was not damaged by the fire of 1146. Within the south transept chapels, however, two mortar floors were recorded, and between them was a thick deposit of burned material, fallen wall-plaster and melted window glass, clear evidence of the fire and the recorded restoration of the church. That building was in its turn overlaid by the standing twelfth-century south transept, which must be part of the church in building in 1154.

At Fountains, the successive rebuildings on the same site can be related to the growth of the community and the growing certainty of economic survival (26). The timber church relates to a period of dreadful uncertainty when it was far from clear whether the community would survive. Its replacement by a modest stone church reflects the stability that came with patronage, and the rebuilding on a vast scale in the 1150s demonstrates the importance of Fountains Abbey as the head of a substantial family of daughter-houses. Its further extension, with the building of an elaborate new eastern arm and eastern transept, creating the Chapel of Nine Altars in the first quarter of the thirteenth century indicates both increasing wealth and liturgical development, only 40 years or so after the great church was completed. Limited excavation has also hinted that there might have been an earlier attempt to enlarge the presbytery before the surviving structure was begun.

An almost parallel development can be seen in the church of the Augustinian canons at Kirkham. The Augustinians were the first reformed order to be settled in England, enjoying the personal patronage of Henry I. Kirkham was the first of three monasteries to be founded by Walter Espec, a courtier and soldier who owed his Yorkshire estates to the Crown. Almost his first act was to establish Kirkham Priory, in about 1120. Ten years later he was to bring the Cistercians to the north, with the foundation of Rievaulx Abbey. The foundation of Rievaulx, and Espec's obvious interest in monastic austerity, had a dramatic effect on the development of Kirkham, which very nearly became a Cistercian abbey with its prior St Waltheof pushing and the patron pulling. The transfer of allegiance went as far as a formal agreement being drawn up in about 1139, although the majority of canons appear not to have accepted the situation. The problem was

resolved in 1143 when Prior Waltheof himself left to join the Cistercian order. The value of the transfer agreement lies in the fact that it describes the monastery as it was at that date: the church was built of squared stone and was covered with shingle, its windows had coloured glass, and a tower is hinted at by the presence of more than one bell. During the consolidation of the site in the 1920s it was discovered that the south wall of the nave and west wall of the south transept contained masonry of two periods of building, and Sir Charles Peers carried out extensive excavations which revealed the ground plans of two twelfth-century churches, as well as the layout of the eastern arm of a projected early-thirteenth-century rebuilding of the whole church which had been abandoned (27). More recent excavation on the north side of the twelfth-century churches and a critical examination of Peers' discoveries, which were never published in full, has allowed the full sequence of events to be understood.

The first church at Kirkham, the one mentioned in the transfer agreement that was never implemented, was a cruciform building of great austerity without aisles and with transepts which do not appear to have had separate eastern chapels. The short presbytery had a square east end. The surviving walls are only 1.2 m (4 ft) thick, suggesting that the building was of modest height, and the south wall of the nave still stands to a height of 1.4 m (4½ ft). The only surviving architectural detail, the base of the eastern processional door to the cloister, would suggest a building date around 1130–40.

This building was almost totally rebuilt on its original ground plan around 1160–70. The walls that butted the cloister on the south side were retained but thickened internally to 1.8 m (6 ft) and the north side of the nave and transept were rebuilt to like width from foundation level. The widening of the walls indicates that they were raised in height, perhaps for an upper tier of windows. Chapels were added to the transepts, and the eastern arm was rebuilt and extended from an original internal length of 13.5 m (44 ft) to just over 18 m (60 ft), its angles supported by clasping buttresses. More remarkably, an axial tower was built at the west end of the nave, a feature paralleled in the recently-excavated early Augustinian church at Gisborough, although there is unequivocal evidence for a tower at the crossing as well, where the stepped plinths of elaborate piers remain.

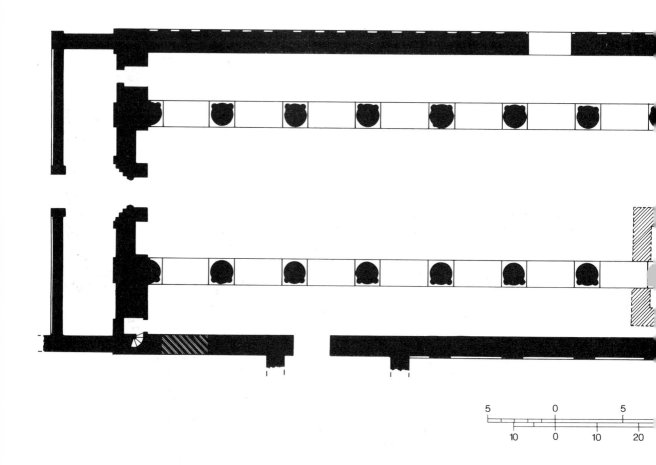

26 *The ground plans of the four churches at Fountains indicate both the growth of the community and its wealth in the first century of the abbey's life.*

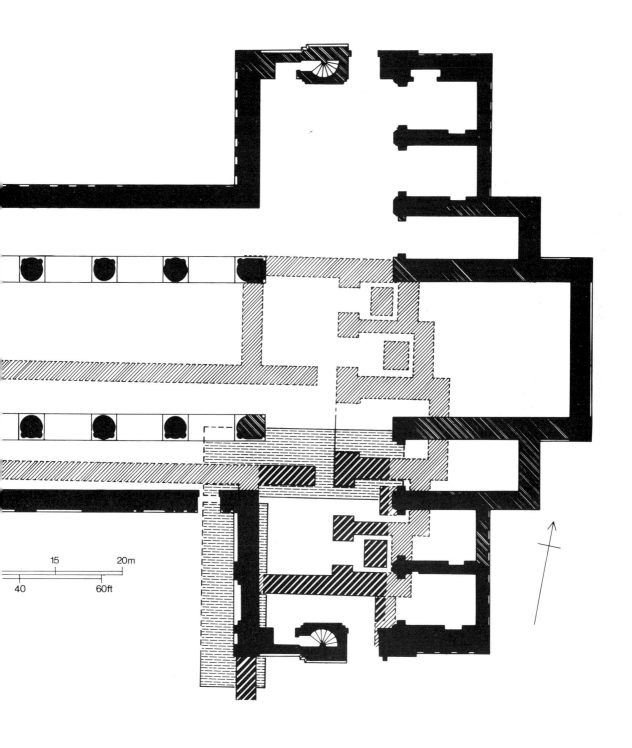

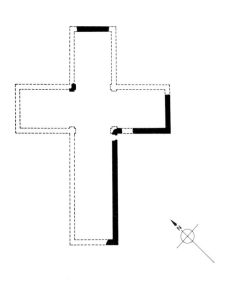

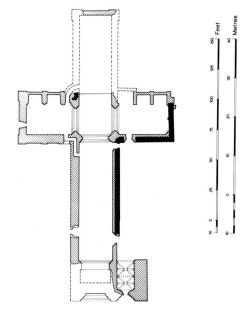

27 *Three churches are known at Kirkham Priory, the earliest a simple cruciform church of the late 1130s, the second a substantial rebuilding of the 1160s or 1170s and the third a monumental rebuilding of the early thirteenth century that was never completed (after Peers).*

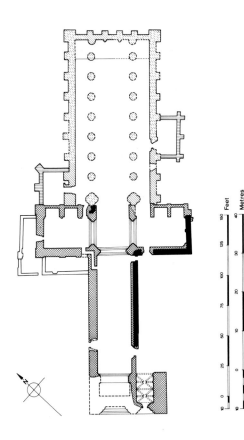

To the south, and of slightly later date, is the vaulted outer parlour and cloister entrance which Peers mistakenly considered to be one of a pair of western towers. Above it is a small chapel, apparently unassociated with the church.

In the first quarter of the thirteenth century, when so many monastic churches were being rebuilt, the canons at Kirkham took the decision to rebuild their church on a much grander scale. The unaisled plan at Kirkham, though common throughout the order, must have seemed very plain and unambitious when compared with the fully-aisled churches of Augustinian Gisborough and Bridlington in Yorkshire. All that was ever completed, however, was an aisled presbytery of eight bays, ending at the west end with a pair of crossing

28 *The form of the early thirteenth century presbytery at Kirkham Priory has been reconstructed from surviving fragments and eighteenth-century drawings by Stuart Harrison.*

piers. From the surviving fragment of its east wall, eighteenth-century drawings and surviving fragments of loose architectural detail, it appears that the new church was going to be one of the finest ever built in the north of England (**28**). The motive for this monumental reconstruction, which was only halted by the eventual lack of money, was the choice of Kirkham as the burial church of the de Roos lords of Helmsley, descendants of the founder Walter Espec. Once the part used by the canons and which contained the patrons' tombs was completed, the scheme was abandoned, leaving one of the most interesting twelfth-century monastic churches in England largely intact.

The third example is the church of the Carthusian charterhouse of Mount Grace (**29**). Begun about 1400 and with three principal phases of building largely represented by standing masonry (**30**), this particular church was developed by accretion rather than rebuilding, the progression of building being apparent in the remaining masonry and confirmed by excavation. In its original state, the priory church was a simple rectangular building 27 m (88 ft) long and 7.7 m (25 ft) wide, divided into two parts by a cross-passage defined by timber screens. Carthusian churches were not

designed for the daily round of services practised by other orders, but were used principally for matins, mass, private mass and vespers. The western part of the church was used by the laybrothers, the eastern part was the monks' choir and the house for the main altar. In 1415 the priory was virtually refounded and the size of the community increased. Within the church this was marked by replacing the screened cross-passage with a pair of stone screen walls that carried a bell-tower, much in the manner of a friars' church, and by extending the monks' choir to the east by a further 9.2 m (30 ft). Sockets in the surviving masonry provide the location of a rood-loft at the east end of the nave with two altars below it, one each side of the tower arch. To the east of the tower, grooves in the side walls of the church and the blocking

29 *Four principal phases of construction can be detected in the surviving fabric of the church at Mount Grace Priory, the first (a) dating to the first years of the fifteenth century, the second (b) to the 1420s, the third (c) belonging to the 1470s and the final phase a burial chapel to the south of the presbytery, in the early sixteenth century.*

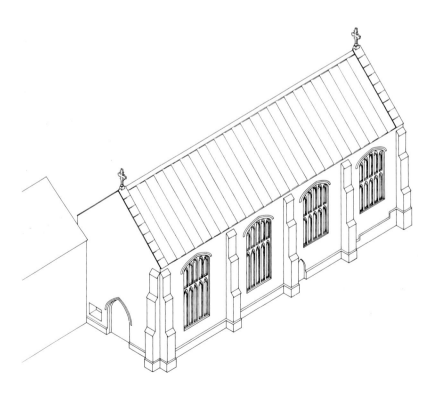

30 *The small church of Mount Grace is the best preserved Carthusian church in England.*

of the lower parts of windows belonging to the original church show the position of the canopies over the monks' stalls, the bases of which were recovered by excavation. This work was financed by Thomas Beaufort, Earl of Dorset, to provide a fitting place for his burial, and his tomb remains in the traditional position of a founder's tomb at the centre of the monks' choir. The success of the Carthusians in the later Middle Ages sprang directly from their strictness of living and was to compromise their yearning for simplicity. The numbers of people who willed their bodies for burial at Mount Grace, hoping that by providing financial support for the community they would aid their own salvation, was far greater than there was space for in the tiny church. Three successive burial chapels were added, greatly increasing the size of the building. The first lay to the south of the nave, built in the third quarter of

the fifteenth century; the second, not much later in date, balanced it on the north side of the nave; and the third, built early in the sixteenth century, lay on the south side of the presbytery. Each contained at least one altar and retains evidence of its fittings. The excavation of the church by St John Hope at the turn of the century, and its re-examination in the early 1960s, recovered much of the missing architectural detail, allowing for accurate reconstruction.

The reconstruction of ruined buildings
Whilst the structure of monastic churches has long been the preserve of architectural historians, archaeology has an important role to play in this field. The study of fallen and displaced masonry recovered by excavation can be of immeasurable value in reconstructing lost or fragmentary elevations. The church at Byland

Abbey, arguably one of the finest English churches built in the twelfth century, was a sadly shattered ruin before it was excavated by Peers in 1922. Previous trenching by Martin Stapylton in about 1820 had recovered large quantities of architectural detail discarded by stone robbers, and Peers, who stripped the whole site, found considerably more. Remarkably little attention has been paid to this collection until recently when Stuart Harrison began its detailed analysis. Relating particular stones to their original findspots using contemporary photographs and surviving site records and by using the critical evidence that remained in the surviving fabric, it proved possible to reconstruct the main elevations of the church which had been lost since the sixteenth century (**colour plate 11**). Furthermore, details of particular elements could be recovered for the first time, showing how the masons had tackled individual parts of the structure. Individual capitals could be identified with their original find-spots and their full forms regenerated from the plans of the piers that supported them. From these the sequence of building could also be identified. Many still survive with evidence of their original painted decoration, which indicates that the apparently plainer forms were originally painted to look at first sight like their more elaborately carved fellows. The accuracy of the reconstruction, being based entirely on the evidence of original structural elements, is such that Byland's role in the development of Gothic architecture can now be reconsidered. The same technique can be applied to many of the ruined or totally buried monastic churches that are currently lost to the archaeological record, and with modern methods of recording more 'lost' churches can be recovered in considerable detail.

Excavation has a critical role to play in the understanding of much more than the physical structure of the monastic church. Churches were not simply open shells, the impression given by their current appearance, but were divided up into distinct units by screens and furniture. However, modern methods of excavation that are capable of recovering the evidence for the development of church use were not applied until the mid-1960s, with the result that painfully little is known about the developing use of the most important of all monastic buildings. A series of excavations designed to reveal the remains of buried monastic sites for public display is at last providing well-researched information that will ultimately transform the perception of the monastic church. The most significant of these large-scale excavations are those of Bordesley Abbey and Norton Priory, though smaller-scale work at sites like Fountains and Haughmond show that there is considerable scope for further work on sites that were thought to be worked-out archaeologically.

The archaeology of liturgy

Bordesley in particular has set new standards for study, aided by the exceptional stratification of no fewer than seven distinct floors ranging in date from the mid twelfth century to the late fifteenth century. To date only the presbytery, crossing, south transept and parts of the nave have been examined (**31**), but the evidence of internal fittings and alterations to the fabric is remarkable. Bordesley was the first site to succeed in defining the connection between structure, decoration, liturgy and burial practice within a much-altered building. In keeping with early Cistercian simplicity, the nave, transepts and choir of the mid-twelfth-century church had earth floors strewn with reeds, and only the presbytery has a floor of lias limestone flags. The choir stalls occupied the two eastern bays of the nave, each bank evidenced by six slots for timber joists. Further slots suggested return stalls for the abbot and prior at the west end of the choir, but there was no evidence of a screen closing off the choir from the nave. The monks entered their choir from its upper entrance in the crossing or through its lower entrance between the western return stalls. A wooden stair in the south transept provided access from the dormitory for night offices.

By the early thirteenth century, the original arrangements were no longer adequate; increasing numbers of monks, changing liturgy, and structural problems all led to modifications. The timber night-stair had been destroyed by fire and was replaced in stone. At the same time, the eastern bay of the nave arcades were blocked with solid walls, and the entrance from the south nave aisle into the transept was under-built, incorporating a narrower archway. Building work of this nature suggests a problem with the crossing, perhaps associated with the addition of a lantern stage

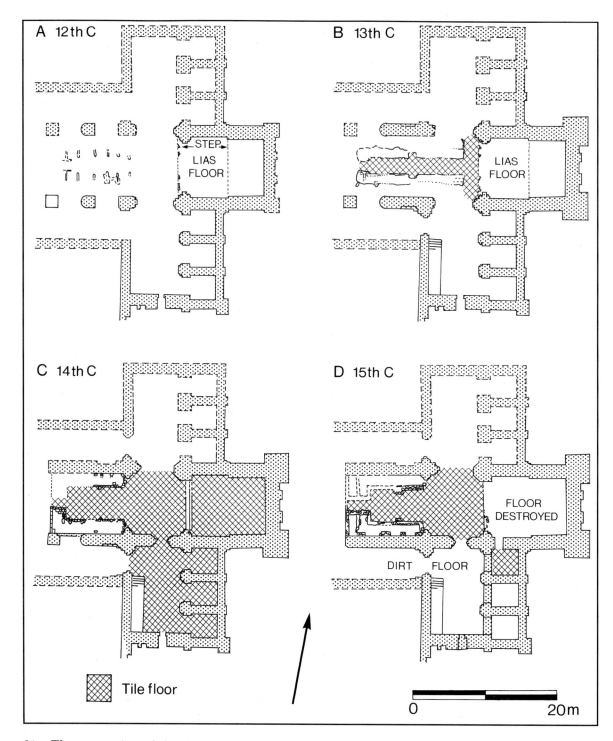

31 *The excavation of the church at Bordesley Abbey has shown how its use and layout varied from the twelfth to the sixteenth century (after Rahtz, Hirst and Wright).*

to the original crossing tower, a fashionable development which flooded the choir with light and was much favoured by the Cistercians in the late twelfth century. Growing numbers required additional stall-space in the choir, and new stalls of two tiers were provided, extending to within 1.8 m (6 ft) of the presbytery step below the crossing. Access to the upper tier of stalls was by way of narrow stairways clearly evidenced in excavation. An oak stall-end from this choir was actually recovered from a later context, showing that the woodwork was severely functional rather than decorative. The earth floors of the transept, crossing, nave aisles and choir were then replaced with a tiled floor, traced by its impressions in the mortar bedding. Wear pattern in the floor showed that the principal entrance to the choir was through the south nave aisle and the lower western entrance. By about 1260–80 the north-west crossing pier was causing concern and needed to be under-built with additional foundations, requiring the removal of the choir stalls. Once these repairs were completed, new stalls were provided on a similar plan and the choir floor renewed with smaller tiles.

The start of the fourteenth century saw further reordering. New choir stalls were again provided, now restricted to the eastern bays of the nave and set on stone plinth-walls. Their provision was associated with the partial blocking of the south crossing arch, leaving little more than a door into the south transept. Obviously the crossing tower was still giving cause for concern. Stone screen walls were also provided in the second bay of the nave arcade to close off the back of the choir stalls, and for the first time the west end of the choir was closed by a timber pulpitum screen set on a stone cill wall. The stalls appear to have been of a single tier and suggest a much-reduced community, a fact demonstrated by the recording of only 34 monks at Bordesley in 1332. It is uncertain whether this reorganization was complete when a catastrophic collapse of the north-west crossing pier occurred, rendering the central area of the church temporarily unusable. The evidence from excavation suggests that the collapse was expected, and that the stalls were removed from the choir before the pier fell, perhaps in the course of repair. The lack of widespread damage or depression of soft floor deposits in the whole of the crossing area might even suggest that the

pier was intentionally felled after the dismantling of superstructure.

The west side of the crossing was then quickly rebuilt, with a new north-west pier and the addition of a matching respond to the surviving south-west pier, the new moulded bases indicating a date around 1330. Builders' rubble and clay was then used to re-level the crossing area, and the choir stalls were replaced on their original cill walls, which had not been seriously disturbed by the reconstruction work. After this, a new tile floor was laid in the whole of the choir, crossing and presbytery. At the end of the fourteenth century the base of the north-east crossing pier was replaced, the tile floor around it being relaid.

About 1400 the church saw a major rebuilding, with the reconstruction of the greater part of the largely unexcavated nave. Perhaps associated with this was a general raising of floor levels by about 30 cm (1 ft) in the south transept and south nave aisle, burying the pier bases and bringing these areas up to the level of the tiled presbytery and crossing. These new floors were not tiled, however, but left as dirt floors. The choir stalls were also replaced at the higher level of the crossing floor and a dirt floor laid there and in the crossing as well. This seemingly retrograde step indicates that there was little concern about the architectural integrity of the structure or concern about the quality of floors in liturgically important areas. The dirt floors might simply be explained by the lack of resources to pay for new tiles. The south transept was in any case ceasing to have any liturgical importance in the course of the fifteenth century and the door in the blocking wall below the south crossing arch was blocked up. In the course of the fifteenth century two of the three eastern chapels of the south transept were also blocked off and abandoned. By about 1470, however, an attempt was made to tidy up the central part of the church, and a new tiled floor was laid in the choir and crossing. Floor levels were considerably raised again, and dirt floors continued in the south nave aisle and south transept until the suppression. The chapels displaced from the south transept were repositioned in the south aisle of the nave.

Although the frequent refloorings seen at Bordesley are perhaps exceptional, excavation has shown that many churches were frequently altered, in terms of both structure and fittings. Improving abbots frequently beautified old but

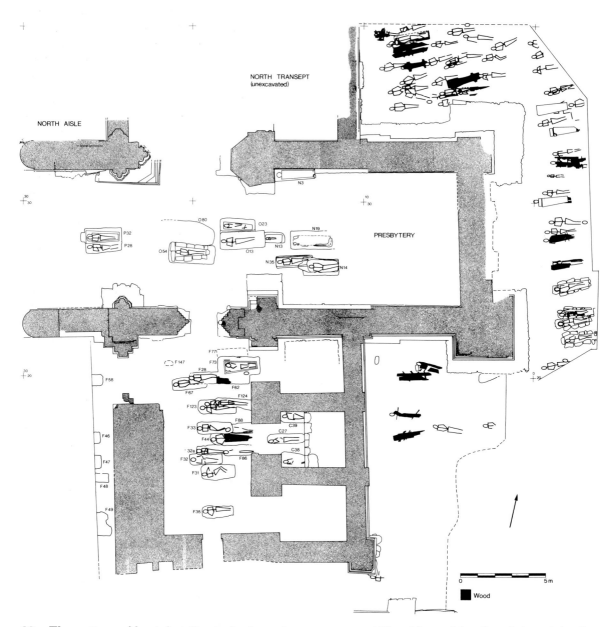

32 *The pattern of burial at Bordesley has also been recovered by excavation, with groups of graves within the church and the convent cemetery outside the building to the east (after Rahtz, Hirst and Wright).*

sound buildings, like John Darnton of Fountains in the 1490s, who inserted great new windows into his church, removed the vaulted ceilings of the eastern parts, reroofed the entire building and divided it up inside with timber

screens still evidenced by the slots cut in the masonry to hold them.

Burials in monastic churches

Though the church was intended solely as a place of prayer for the religious, it was seen by patronal families in a different light. They founded monasteries for the benefit of their souls, and, though most orders were initially reluctant to see their churches taken over as burial places for the laity, they were prepared to grant sepulture to their founders. Pressure from outsiders grew throughout the Middle Ages, and so too did the temptation to accept the benefactions that went with burials. Apart from founders, who were buried in the midst of the choir, few laymen were buried in monastic churches before the thirteenth century, and, as the superiors were normally buried in the chapter-house, twelfth-century churches were rarely used for burial because of the disruption they caused to floors. That situation did not last, and, as chapter-houses filled up and benefactors pressed, monastic churches became mausolea as well as houses of prayer.

With a good stratified sequence of floors and liturgical replanning, it is possible to study the development of burial practice within the church at Bordesley (32). The earliest burials start in the early thirteenth century in the south transept and late thirteenth century in the crossing. The earliest graves in the south transept were a group of three in the central chapel, and one to its west. By the late fifteenth century a further nine graves had been dug before the entrance to this chapel, and the impression given by the group of burials is that it is a family grouping. A smaller group outside the northern chapel also had its origins in the thirteenth century. The transept burials were, with a single exception, either uncoffined or buried in wooden coffins. A single stone coffin occurred at the entrance to the northern chapel, implying a better quality of burial. The burials in the choir, crossing and presbytery were generally of a better quality, with two stone coffins and one built grave. Their central position at the focus of the choir suggests important patrons, and the centrally placed grave in the presbytery which had evidence of a raised tomb above it has been tentatively identified as that of Guy Beauchamp, Earl of Warwick, who was buried at Bordesley in 1315.

33 *A group of four grave markers from the church at Monk Bretton, (a) a priest's grave marked by a chalice, (b) the marker of brother Osbert de Gresby, (c) a knight's marker, and (d) a plain floriate cross.*

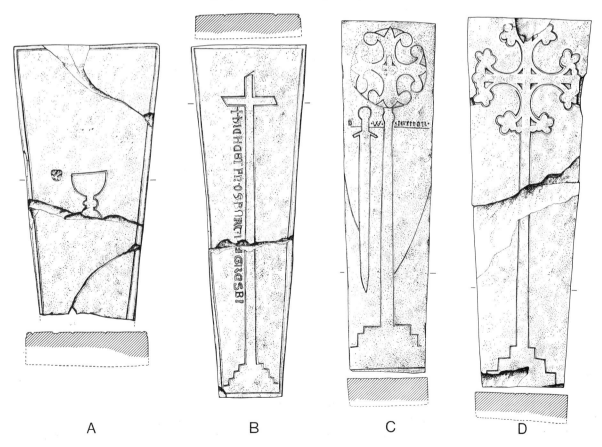

A   B   C   D

Again, there are groupings by either family or tenurial association.

Although Norton Priory lacked the deep stratification of Bordesley, it did produce good evidence of burial practice relating to its patronal families. The development of a chapel to the north of the presbytery and entered from the north transept appears to have taken place to provide both a lady chapel and a burial place for the Duttons, the dominant benefactors of the priory from the thirteenth century (see 37). Their earlier burials were for the most part in stone coffins with fine carved lids. Later burials, some filling gaps within the earlier stone coffins, were in wooden coffins, their graves marked by tile panels or effigies. Elsewhere, grave markers are common survivors, one of the finest collections remaining in the floor of the nave at Bardney Abbey (see 9). These are particularly fine, not only representing local families and abbots but also marking the graves of common monks and their families, a late medieval practice to judge from the dates the slabs record. More commonly, less elaborate grave markers are the rule. Within the flagstone floor of the priory church at Monk Bretton are 14 simple grave markers, commemorating both benefactors and monks (33). One simply marked with a chalice is that of a priest, the grave below which was found to contain a pewter mortuary chalice during the excavation of the site in 1923–6, whilst that of Brother Osbert de Gresby has a plain cross, probably a standard pattern bought from the quarry, with an added inscription filled with lead. A shield and sword, with added inscription, commemorates a knightly burial.

A note of caution should be added, especially at Monk Bretton where some of the stones have their foot-ends to the west. Grave slabs were frequently moved and used as paving. One marker at Thornholme Priory had been relaid when the north transept was refloored, and the associated grave cut did not lie directly beneath it. Grave effigies must have been a common sight in monastic churches, with fine collec-

tions surviving at Furness Abbey and the London Temple, but for the most part they are found only as broken fragments. Their loss is made good partly by documentary references: the graves of the de Roos patrons of Kirkham Priory for instance are described in a family genealogy as being made of marble and their locations recorded where there are now empty graves.

The graves of the religious were normally found in a cemetery to the east or north of the church and usually segregated from lay burials. Few monastic cemeteries have been studied in any detail, the most important exception being that at Bordesley where a small area to the east of the presbytery has now been examined (see 32). In all, 128 burials have been excavated, including at least three females and five children. The burials could be phased by the interleaving of construction deposits associated with the church itself. The earliest, which were all male and presumably religious, were particularly interesting. Though the bodies were uncoffined, they were covered with pieces of reused timber which appear to have come from a building. One piece gave a dendrochronological date of 1150 ± 9, leading to the speculation that the earliest members of the community were buried below fragments of their foundation-period timber church. Later burials were found in built stone graves, wooden coffins, or marked with stone slabs. Excavation to the north of the nave at Whitby in 1924 revealed an extensive cemetery overlaying the remains of the preconquest monastery and displaying many of the same burial techniques. In that case, the skeletal material was not studied and probably remains *in situ*.

What is desperately needed today is the large-scale study of the total burial practice of any religious house where lay burials can be separated from those of the convent, and be sorted by date. Only in this way will we be able to get a clear impression of one of the most important aspects of religious life, the monastery as a mausoleum.

3

The cloister

Monasteries for men and women who had withdrawn from the world to serve God in a disciplined round of prayer required not only a church but also a series of domestic buildings designed for a communal and enclosed life. From the tenth century, English monasteries followed the continental example of arranging their domestic buildings around a central courtyard or cloister, itself the innermost enclosure of the precinct. The very word cloister was derived from the Latin *claustrum*, which literally means a door-bolt or lock and amplifies the restricted access to the 'monks' house'.

Although many monastic communities had lived communally since the foundation of St Basil's monastery of Neocaesaria in about 360, a concept which had spread slowly to western Europe and which was to be encapsulated in the rule that St Benedict drew up for his monastery of Monte Casino after 529, there was no regulated pattern of building that dictated the layout of domestic buildings on early monastic sites. In England, two separate monastic traditions derived from Mediterranean sources were introduced; one from Ireland, the other introduced by St Augustine's Roman mission to Kent. No domestic buildings connected with St Augustine's churches at Canterbury are known from before the eighth century. In the north of England, however, three sites have provided a tantalizing glimpse of the domestic arrangements of major Saxon monasteries.

The domestic buildings of Saxon monasteries

St Hild's double monastery of Whitby, founded in 657, was partially excavated in the 1920s (**34**). Though the method of excavation was brutal by modern standards, all the archaeological deposits being dug away to expose masonry walls, drains and paving left on top of

low banks of natural clay, and few of the finds being adequately recorded, a large area of complicated structures was recorded stone by stone. Whitby was a double monastery for men and women of a type more common on the Continent, important enough to be the scene in 664 of the synod at which the Roman tradition became firmly established in the north. Although more than 0.4 ha (1 acre) of the site was examined between 1920 and 1925, it would appear that the main buildings of the Saxon abbey lie below the church and cloister of the later medieval house and remain to be excavated. Critical study by Rosemary Cramp and Philip Rahtz of what is known has enabled the partial interpretation of the site. Analysis of the finds indicates that the buildings recovered appear to lie in the women's part of the monastery, and that there are at least two and possibly more phases of development, the earliest with timber buildings evidenced by burned daub, replaced by stone-built structures. The buildings are not a series of free-standing structures but elaborate 'ranges' of rooms served by a complicated network of drains and divided into groups by pathways. The remains of individual buildings are in many cases fragmentary, and most show some evidence of modification and reconstruction. In spite of this, several elements can be identified with a reasonable degree of certainty. Individual cells each comprising a living room with an open hearth and a bedroom with a latrine can be recognized at A, B, C and D, whilst E was originally identified as a store or guest-house, the finds from it suggesting that either use was possible. It was at least partially rebuilt when a series of rooms, H, was built onto its east side. To the west, a series of structures overlay earlier burials and appear to date from the early years of the ninth century. Room F, perhaps part of a heavily

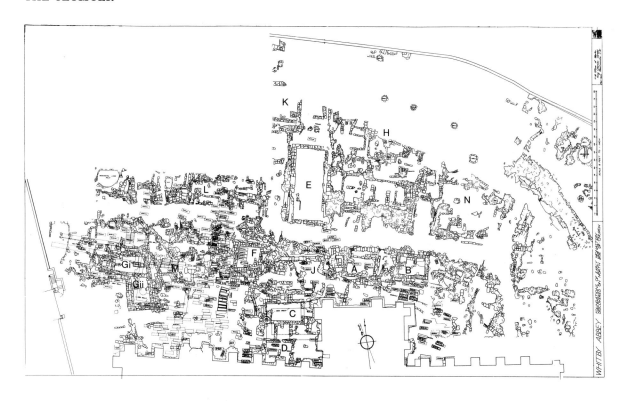

34 *Excavation by Peers and Radford revealed the extensive remains of pre-conquest buildings on the north side of the Norman and later abbey church at Whitby. The plan is one of the earliest instances of stone-by-stone recording.*

robbed building extending to the west, was domestic in nature, producing *styli*, needles, pins and a quern. Further west still a pair of rooms, G1 and G2, produced 18 loom-weights, indisputable evidence of weaving. The more fragmentary range, L, to the north of this area, contained a series of rooms used, judging from the artifacts they contained, for spinning, writing, copying and reading. No obviously communal dormitory, refectory, or room for chapter meetings, all central to religious life, has so far been identified at Whitby or at the recently excavated contemporary monastery of Hartlepool. However, Bede, writing of the contemporary monastery of Coldingham, described how the monastery contained both public and private cells and buildings for study and reading.

The picture developed at Whitby can be further extended by the more recent excavations at Monkwearmouth and Jarrow conducted by Rosemary Cramp. At Whitby, the area examined lay to the north of the monastic church or churches. At both Monkwearmouth and Jarrow, excavation took place on the other side of the church, producing evidence of the buildings not yet seen at Whitby. In both cases, the south side of the church was bordered by a cemetery, used at least in part for lay burials. Both monasteries were established by Benedict Biscop, a Northumbrian noble who had been professed monk at the island monastery of Lerins, travelled widely on the Continent, and had been temporarily abbot of St Peter and St Paul at Canterbury. Monkwearmouth was founded in 674, Jarrow in 682, Biscop sought masons and glaziers in Gaul, and it is fair to assume that his two monasteries reflected contemporary continental models.

At Monkwearmouth (**35**), excavation failed to locate major communal buildings, but did give tantalizing clues as to how the monastery was laid out. A corridor-like structure, with glazed windows and a slated roof, led south from the church, perhaps an enclosed 'cloister' giving access to the communal buildings, for

35 *The saxon buildings to the south of the church at Monkwearmouth (after Cramp).*

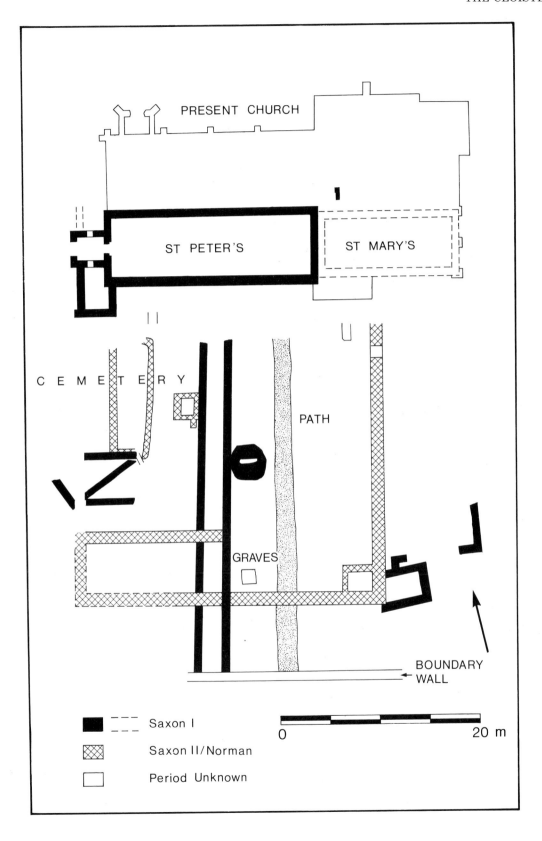

PRESENT CHURCH

ST PETER'S

ST MARY'S

CEMETERY

PATH

GRAVES

BOUNDARY
WALL

Saxon I

Saxon II/Norman

Period Unknown

0   20 m

the historian Bede, who was a monk of Wearmouth, specifically refers to a cloister there. To its east a cobbled path also led to the church through the cemetery. These primary structures were later truncated by a wall, which in origin was apparently of pre-conquest date but reused in the eleventh century recolonization of the site. Sadly the post-conquest redevelopment of the site and the restricted area available for study make it impossible to recover the precise details of the early monastery.

At Jarrow, however, in spite of post-conquest reconstruction, Professor Cramp was able to recover good evidence of the form and layout of the monastic buildings (36). The area to the south of the church was terraced, and on these terraces major stone buildings were recovered. Some 16 m (52 ft) south of the church, and sharing its east-west alignment, were two substantial structures, A and B, with walls of coursed masonry laid in mortar and faced with plaster. Both had been destroyed by fire. Building A comprised a range of two rooms, each with a floor of Roman style *opus signinum*. In the centre of the eastern room was an octagonal base associated with fragments of a shaft carved with heavy plant scrolls, interpreted by the excavator as the remains of a stone lectern. It seems likely that this room, enlarged by the ultimate removal of the cross-wall, was the monks' refectory. To the south was an annex which had a partially paved floor at a lower level than the main building with pebble-lined settings which might have been for standing large barrels or storage vessels. It appears to have been added after the demolition of the cross-wall in Building A and was the servery associated with the refectory. A small hut found to the south of Building A appears to have been a workshop associated with the building of the servery, for it contained quantities of Roman tile which was used as chippings in the flooring of the new work. Separated by a flagged path from Building A was Building B, a range of one large and two small rooms. The larger room had the setting for a seat against its east wall and a circular tank or well placed centrally at its west end. Fragments of plain and coloured glass found along the south wall indicate that it had glazed windows of the highest quality. Finds included a *stylus*, a pin with a ring-and-dot head and a small whetstone, suggesting that the room had been used as a place of

assembly and writing, what would have been the 'chapter-house' of a later monastery. The two rooms to the east, in comparison, were not 'public' but comprised a small oratory with an *opus signinum* floor and the base of an altar against its east wall, divided by a timber screen set in a slotted stone base from a living room with a sink in its south-east corner. This suite can be compared with the individual cells identified at Whitby, but at Jarrow it is associated with one of the public buildings of the monastery very much in the contemporary fashion of domestic halls and private lordly accommodation. Almost certainly it was the accommodation of the abbot or a senior monk.

The late-Roman style buildings of the upper terrace at Jarrow were supplemented by wooden buildings on the lower terrace. Several wattle huts produced evidence of glass-working, and there was evidence that the lower terrace was also cultivated. At its east end was a partially excavated stone building, D, again with painted plaster on its inner wall surfaces and producing some 900 fragments of plain and coloured window glass. Its latest use was as a workshop, but its primary use was perhaps a guest-house, placed as it was close to the river and away from the monastic buildings. From Bede's written description we know that other buildings await discovery, including a common dormitory, the kitchen and the bakehouse.

The development of the cloister

The formal development of a cloister – that is, a square garth on one side of the church surrounded by ranges of buildings used only by the religious – began on the Continent, and by the early ninth century was sufficiently established to be used as a model for a major Benedictine monastery in the St Gall plan. The introduction of the enclosed cloister to England was part of the mid-tenth-century reform of monastic practice centred on St Dunstan. The *Regularis Concordia* mentions the provision of a common refectory, a common dormitory, the cloister itself, a room set apart for daily chapter meetings, a warming-house, a kitchen, a bakehouse and a guest-house. This grouping of buildings into a central nucleus was the next stage on from the development of sites such as Whitby and Jarrow, both of which would have been reordered on this pattern if they had not been destroyed by the Viking raids of the later ninth century. It was to remain the standard

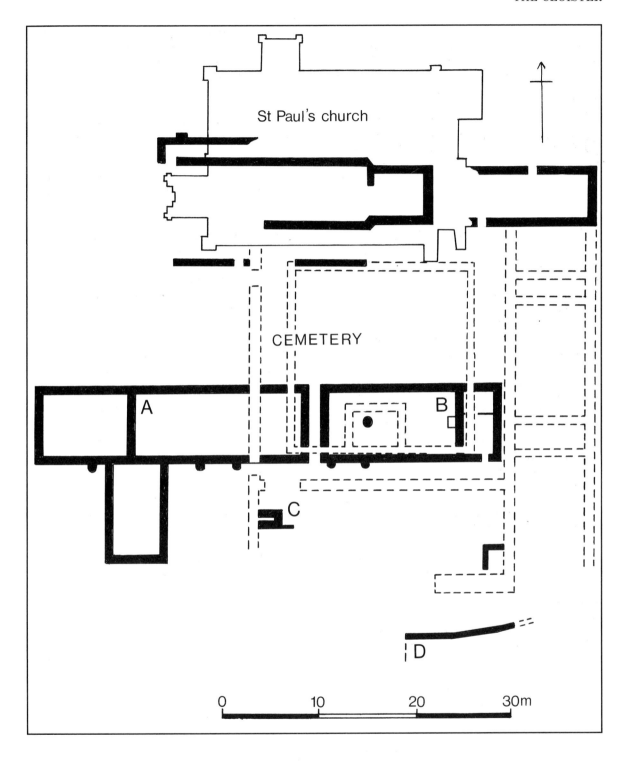

St Paul's church

CEMETERY

A

B

C

D

0   10   20   30m

36 *Excavation at Jarrow below the cloister ranges of the post-conquest monastery have revealed extensive remains of Benedict Biscop's domestic ranges separated from his churches by a cemetery (after Cramp).*

monastic plan up to the early years of the sixteenth century.

The earliest cloister in England to have been identified by excavation was that of St Dunstan's own monastery of Glastonbury, to the south of the church and separated from it by a cemetery. The east range was aligned on the south porticus of the church (see **18**). The cloister garth itself measured some 55 by 37 m (180 by 120 ft) and was surrounded on three sides by ranges from 6 to 8 m (20 to 26 ft) wide. Sadly little is known about the planning of the ranges. At Canterbury, however, excavation below the post-conquest cloister of St Augustine's Abbey has revealed the layout of not one but two late Saxon cloisters on the north side of the church (see **15**). Although their plan is only fragmentary, it is possible to identify the earlier layout as that of Abbot Aelfmaer built between 1006 and 1017, now firmly attached to the church and with ranges of rooms on all three sides. It was enlarged, with the east range aligned on the rotunda which Abbot Wulfric left unfinished on his death in 1059. Presumably Wulfric was also responsible for the enlargement of the cloister. At Westminster, Edward the Confessor provided a cloister attached to the south side of the nave of his new church built in the Norman manner which was to become the standard layout for all subsequent English monasteries.

The layout of the cloister ranges

The plan of the domestic buildings of a medieval monastery was rapidly becoming standardized, and remarkably little variation in layout occurs despite the observances of particular orders. The placing of the domestic buildings to the north or south of the church was as much controlled by the access to drainage and a water supply as by any other preference, though there was a marked tendency to put them on the sheltered southern side. Nuns' houses seem, however, to have preferred to build their cloister to the north of the church. At the Benedictine nunnery of Wilberfoss (see **20**), for instance, the cloister buildings described in 1535 would have been instantly recognizable to the first generation of nuns who colonized the site in 1153.

Item the cloyster [A] at the northe syde of churche conteyneth in length lx ffoote square, and in bredith vj ffoote w^{t}out any glasse, and chambres over iij partes therof, and the iiijth parte coueryd w^t slates.

Item the chapiter house [B] at th' est parte of the cloyster new made, xx foote long and xvj foote brode, seylid aboue and plasterid, and goode substancyalle tymber walles, whitlymed, a glasse wyndow conteyning viij foote of glasse.

Item the mylke house [C], xij foote long and viij foote brode, and tymber walles w^{t}out glasse.

Item an other litle chambre or store house [D], viij foote s(quare).

Item the gyle house [E] viij foote square, w^{t}out glasse, tymber walles.

Item a fayer new chambre [F] ouer the chapiter house, xx foote long and xvi foote brode, goode substancialle tymber walles, seylid and plasterid aboue; a baye wyndow glasid, conteyning xij foote of glasse and coueryd w^t slates; a chymney.

Item a little closett by the same [G] for to loke into the churche to hear seruyse.

Item the dorter [H] ouer the chapiter house and cloyster and other (chambers, ...) foot long, (...) foote brode, tymber walles, and coueryd w^t slates.

Item the kychin [I] at the northest corner of the cloyster, vij foote square w^t a chymney, tymber walles, and coueryd w^t slates.

Item one new larder house [J] by the kychyn vnder the garner, xiiij foote longe and ix foote brode, tymber walles.

Item an other inner larder house [K], xiiij foote long and xj foote brode, w^t new tymber walles, whitlymed and under the garnar.

Item the low halle [L] at the north parte of the cloyster, xxiiij foote longe and xviij foote brode, tymber walles w^{t}out any glasse.

Item a buttrye [M] xviij foote long and viij foote brode.

Item a fayer new chambre ouer the halle [N], xxx foote longe and xxj foote brode, welle seilid and plasterid aboue and coueryd w^t slates, ij baye wyndows glasid conteyning

37 *The excavated plan of the church and cloister at Norton Priory showing (a) the layout of the first stone buildings, (b) an enlargement of the buildings that reflects a growing community, and (c) the final late-medieval planning of the house that implies greater comfort for a reduced population (after Greene).*

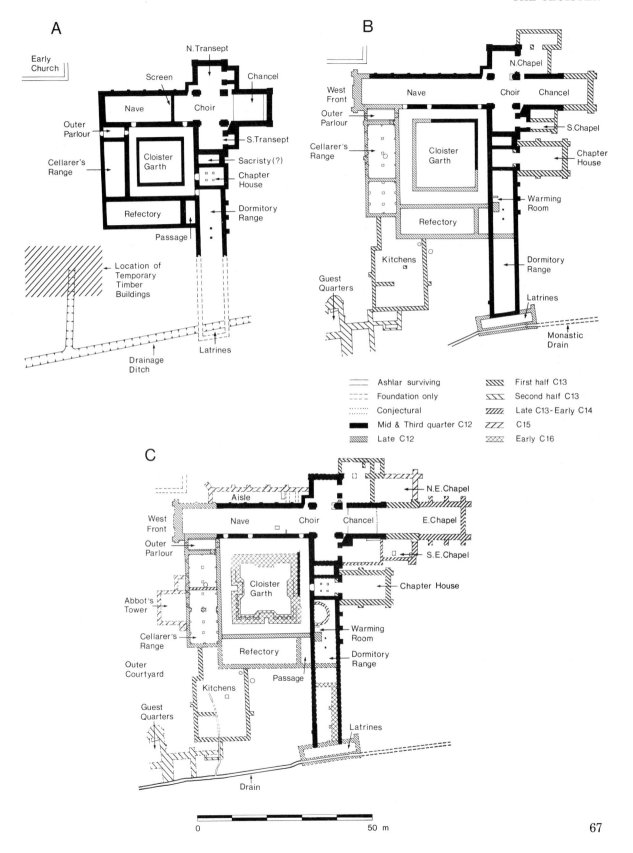

A

Early Church

N. Transept

Screen

Chancel

Nave

Choir

Outer Parlour

S. Transept

Sacristy (?)

Cellarer's Range

Cloister Garth

Chapter House

Refectory

Dormitory Range

Passage

Location of Temporary Timber Buildings

Latrines

Drainage Ditch

B

N. Chapel

West Front

Nave

Choir

Chancel

Outer Parlour

S. Chapel

Cellarer's Range

Chapter House

Cloister Garth

Warming Room

Refectory

Dormitory Range

Kitchens

Guest Quarters

Latrines

Monastic Drain

Ashlar surviving
Foundation only
Conjectural
Mid & Third quarter C12
Late C12

First half C13
Second half C13
Late C13-Early C14
C15
Early C16

C

Aisle

N.E. Chapel

West Front

Nave

Choir

Chancel

E. Chapel

Outer Parlour

S.E. Chapel

Abbot's Tower

Chapter House

Cloister Garth

Cellarer's Range

Warming Room

Outer Courtyard

Refectory

Dormitory Range

Kitchens

Passage

Guest Quarters

Latrines

Drain

0   50 m

xxiiij foote of glasse, and a chymney.

Item a little buttrye by the same [O].

Item a low parler [P] at the norwest corner of the cloyster, xvj foote square, w^t a baye wyndow glasid conteyning xij foote of glasse, a chymney, the floore bourded, seilid aboue and plasterid and payntid and tymber walles.

Item a little buttrye by the same [Q].

Item ane other buttrye at ane other syde of the same [R].

Item a litle kychyn [S] by the said parler w^t a fayer chymney.

Item a chambre ouer the said parler [T], xvj foote square, seilid and pargett aboue, coueryd w^t slates, a baye wyndow glasid conteyning vj foote of glasse, and a chymney.

Item ane other chamber by the same [U], xvj foote longe and xij foote brode, seilid aboue and coueryd w^t slates.

Item ane other chambre ouer the west parte of the cloyster [V], xvj foote longe and xij foote brode, coueryd w^t slates, tymber walles, w^{t}oute glasse.

Item iij other chambers ouer the west parte of the cloyster [W], coueryd w^t slates, w^{t}out glasse.

Item iij litle houses vndir the same [X] to ley woode yn.

Although Wilberfoss was a poor nunnery built predominantly of timber, it provided the same facilities for the community as the richer stone-built monasteries: cloister, chapter-house, dormitory, refectory and kitchen, and accommodation for its president. Relaxing monastic discipline might have made the buildings more comfortable than they were originally, and certainly provided space for private use in place of the open ranges favoured in the eleventh and twelfth centuries, often marked by the provision of fireplaces in ranges that were not originally heated.

Although cloister ranges survive in varying degrees of completeness on many sites, few have been extensively excavated under modern conditions and the greater part of our knowledge comes from exploration in the late nineteenth and early twentieth centuries. An important exception is the Augustinian priory of Norton, a house of reasonably modest means. Excavated for public display between 1971 and 1983, the whole of the claustral area was examined (**37**). The significance of Norton is that it demonstrates the growth of a small and

relatively simple house over four centuries. The first buildings were of timber, and lay outside the area of the permanent stone cloister buildings, a reminder that stone monasteries took some time to build and that the founding community required temporary buildings to continue religious life before their new buildings were finished. The first permanent stone buildings provided were typical of a small monastery. The east range contained the monks' common dormitory over a sacristy which also doubled as a library, the chapter-house where daily business was conducted and discipline administered, and a long undercroft, the day room, often given over to study and manual work. The south range had a passage at its east end and otherwise contained the refectory or dining hall, often at first-floor level above an undercroft. The west range which closed the cloister from the Inner Court contained the outer parlour and cellarage on the ground floor with accommodation for the prior and guests above. The cloister was enlarged following a growth of the community in the late twelfth century, the south range and west range being rebuilt beyond their original sites. This growth continued into the thirteenth century, with the building of a new chapter-house and kitchens, followed by the provision of guest accommodation outside the cloister. This last development would suggest that the prior's quarters in the west range of the cloister were growing, a process which was to continue into the fifteenth century with the construction of a tower against the west wall of the range. Little remains above ground apart from the lower storey of the rebuilt west range which was incorporated in a post-suppression house, and without excavation this complicated sequence of development would never have become apparent.

There is no reason to suspect that Norton Priory is exceptional in the way its cloister buildings grew and were modified, though the provision of major stone ranges and an enclosed cloister often took a considerable time to develop, as surviving ruins testify. At Fountains Abbey, the earliest buildings were of timber and do not appear to have been built around a court, though these were rapidly replaced by stone buildings of standard layout which were modified and extended repeatedly throughout the second half of the twelfth century. Large and wealthy communities were

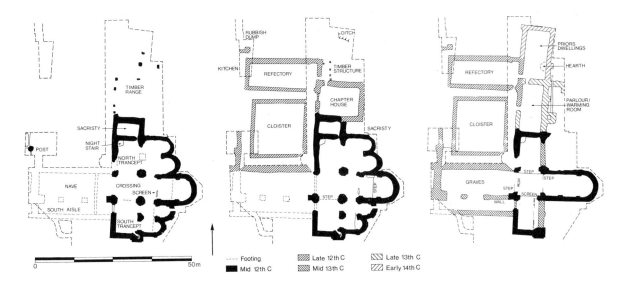

---- Footing   ▨ Late 12th C   ▨ Late 13th C

■ Mid 12th C   ▨ Mid 13th C   ▨ Early 14th C

38 *At Sandwell Priory, building was remarkably slow with progression from (a) a part-built church and timber domestic range of the mid twelfth century, through (b) regular cloister ranges of early thirteenth century date, to a simplified layout (c) which dates from the early fourteenth century (after Hodder).*

able to provide themselves with permanent buildings within a few years of foundation.

But this was not so for many of the small houses that make up the bulk of England's medieval monastic settlement. Few small houses have ever been studied archaeologically, distorting the picture of cloister development in favour of richer establishments which make up the bulk of sites with surviving structure. An important exception is the Benedictine priory of Sandwell (**38**). There excavation has shown that the earlier buildings, dated by tree-rings in surviving timbers to a felling-date of 1159–60, comprised the eastern parts of an unfinished church and a timber domestic range to its north. There was no formal cloister garth. The building of stone domestic ranges did not begin until the end of the twelfth century, when the timber domestic range was replaced by a stone chapter-house with a dormitory above it. A cloister was established, perhaps 40 years after the foundation, enclosed to the north by a new refectory and kitchen, and on the west by a wall. The north wall of the nave must have been built to complete the enclosure. Developments from the mid thirteenth century

to the first quarter of the fourteenth century, included the completion of the church. Within the cloister, the chapter-house was demolished, to be replaced with a heated room that served as warming-house, day-room and parlour, with a new dormitory above it. A small latrine tower against its east wall was the first evidence of the sanitary arrangements normally provided in the earliest years of a monastery's life (see Chapter 5). To the north, the remainder of the range, built before 1330, was the prior's lodging, with a heated ground-floor hall and a chamber at first-floor level connecting with the dormitory. It had taken the tiny community at Sandwell approximately 150 years to provide the ranges of buildings required by their rule, and even then their provision was basic.

The cloister alleys

Excavation alone cannot show how cloister buildings developed, for it provides only ground plans and building contents. It is necessary to combine it with a study of surviving masonry and loose elements recovered from individual sites if a full picture of cloister buildings is to be recovered. This is particularly true for the cloister itself, the heart of the monastery, and especially its alleys that linked all the cloister buildings and the church. The cloister alleys were the monks' workplace, used for writing and study as well as meditation, and surviving cloisters such as Gloucester and Norwich show that they were places of great beauty. Few survive in place, their fragile structures being amongst the first to collapse when the monastic buildings were unroofed, but clearance and excavation have revealed considerable quantities of fallen stonework which is capable of reconstruction. At Roche Abbey, for instance, the cloister arcade built in 1170–80 survived until the suppression. Typical of the majority of English cloister arcades, it was open to the weather, supported on twin shafts with easily identified bases and capitals. Recent study of the fragments recovered by nineteenth-century excavation and clearance work of the 1920s has enabled its reconstruction (**39**). Remarkably, it shows a change in design part way along one alley, neither the masons nor the monks seemingly concerned about its radical change of form. Heavily moulded towards the garth, it was plain on its inner face, and the whole was

painted white inside and out, with perhaps the detailing of the capitals outlined in red.

Designed for the warmer climate of continental Europe, the open cloister, just like that of the poor nuns at Wilberfoss, must have been cold and cheerless in winter. From the fourteenth century there was an increasing tendency to replace the open arcades with glazed windows or to fit wooden frames into old arcades to permit their glazing, for the cloister alleys were not simply corridors linking the

39 *The cloister arcade from Roche Abbey, begun about 1170, survives as many fragments recovered by excavation which are capable of reconstruction (G. Coppack and S. Harrison).*

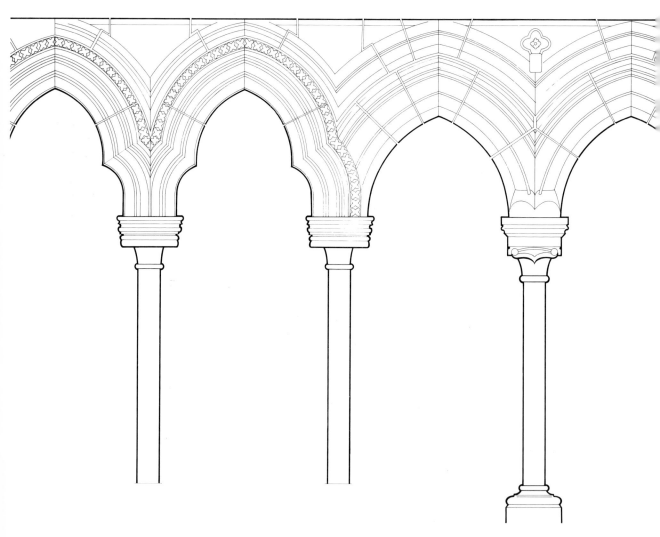

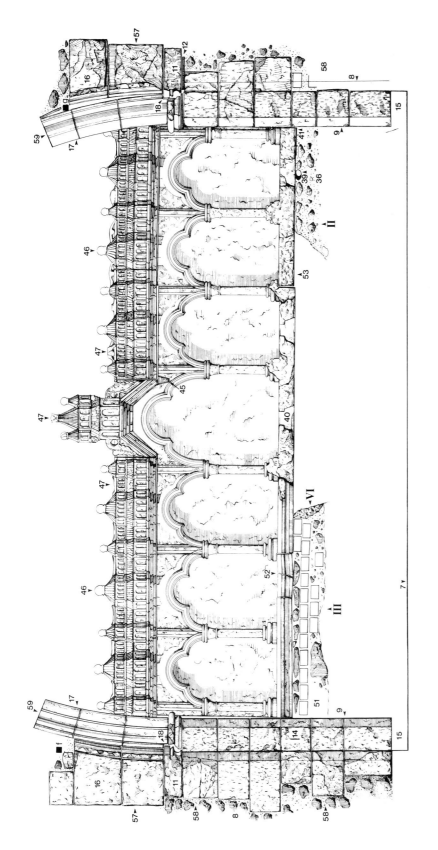

SOUTHWICK PRIORY

40 *The lavatorium at Southwick Priory, revealed when its post-medieval brick blocking was removed (J. Thorn).*

71

communal buildings with the church but the very heart of monastic life. The alley against the church was traditionally allotted to the religious for reading, study and the copying of manuscripts, with the provision of desks or carrels. At Rievaulx these were of timber, whilst in the greatest houses like Gloucester and Chester they were an integral part of the stone alley walls. A wall bench might be provided against the church as well. Books were kept in the east alley, either in small lockers or purpose-built libraries such as the three bay structure that still survives at Much Wenlock. The east alley was normally kept clear of fittings as it was the principal access to the church from the cloister ranges, but it was also a common burial place for patrons, especially in front of the chapter-house. The alley opposite the church and fronting the refectory normally contained the laver or washing place and was thus provided with piped water and drains (see Chapter 5). It was commonly used by the religious as a laundry, fitted up with wooden tubs and strung with washing-lines. In houses of Augustinian canons where the laver might be placed in the west alley, that alley might also be used for washing. In many houses, the west alley of the cloister, not regularly used by the choir-monks, was used for the training of novices.

The laver itself, placed near to the refectory door, was architecturally distinguished to emphasize its spiritual and social importance, and was the most elaborate feature of the cloister. Few were as fine as that provided for the Augustinian canons at Southwick (**40**). A fine Purbeck marble screen with seven canted niches capped by a frieze of aisled and pyramid-roofed structures was set within a tall arch inserted into the cloister wall of the refectory range, though it was not originally made to be used in that location. The panels that made up the screen had originally been held together with iron cramps, all of which had been removed before it was reused in the construction of the laver, and the screen itself may originally have been made as the setting for an altar. Later disturbance had removed the trough that occupied the lower part of the recess, but it is known from sixteenth-century sources that it was made of pewter, presumably within a stone surround. In the floor of each niche is a socket for a tap, and pipe-chases can be traced in the inner wall of the refectory

bringing water to the laver.

Cloister buildings

The chapter-house, which was normally to be found in the east range of the cloister buildings, was the place where discipline was maintained and corporate business discussed. Accordingly, it was a room that displayed the importance of the house. Normally it was vaulted, the roof being carried on pillars as at Cistercian Jervaulx (**colour plate 8**). Wall-benches were provided for the monks, whilst the president's seat was against the east wall. At his feet were the graves of his predecessors, and such was the desire for abbots to be buried in the chapter-house that they were crammed in tight rows. Nowhere is this clearer than at Fountains Abbey where 19 abbots were buried between 1170 and 1346 after which no suitable space remained and the abbots chose instead to be buried in the church. By the head of Abbot Robert of Pipewell's grave is a socketed stone that marks the position of a lectern, a standard fitting of the chapter-house, for it gets its name from the daily reading of a chapter of the rule of St Benedict. At Byland Abbey, excavation in the 1920s recovered the base of a free-standing lectern and also the great communal ink-pot used there for the signing of the deed of surrender in 1539 (**41**).

The dormitory regularly occupied the first floor of the east range, so placed that it had easy access to the choir. Its location was further controlled by the need to provide adequate drainage for an associated latrine-block. Its

41 *The sixteenth-century pottery inkwell found in the chapter-house at Byland Abbey.*

placing in the west range at Durham, Easby and Worcester seems to have resulted simply from the location of suitable drainage and the topography of the site. At Benedictine Durham and Westminster, the dormitories retain their medieval roofs and give some idea of the scale of the building, but nowhere do the internal partitions survive that divided the dormitory into individual cubicles. At Jervaulx, the sockets that held the wooden screens between the cubicles can still be seen (42) and have every appearance of dating to the early years of the thirteenth century. Similar sockets can be seen in the laybrothers' dormitory in the west range at Fountains Abbey in a building dating to the 1170s.

Below the dormitory, apart from the chapter-house, there were usually three other spaces, normally vaulted, which were entered from the cloister. The first was the parlour where talking was permitted for limited periods. At Thornton Abbey it was placed exceptionally between the church and chapter-house, a cheerless room with wall-benches and an earth floor (43). The second was a simple passage through the range leading to the infirmary which was provided for sick and ageing monks, who still required access to the church and chapter-house. The third space was normally a large room, often called simply the dormitory undercroft and sometimes thought to have been used by the novices. Little is known about this room, and in sixteenth-century surveys and valuations it is often overlooked or called a 'chamber' which is far from helpful. At Rievaulx Abbey, Peers excavated such a room in 1921–4 that still contained the fallen remains of its vault sealing the contents of the room. Iron rings hanging from the keystones of the vault indicate that the room was lit by hanging lights in every

42 The west wall of the dormitory range survives almost to full height at Jervaulx Abbey, and sockets between the windows are thought to be the fixings for the timber partitions of individual cubicles or cells. They were provided when the wall was built at the beginning of the thirteenth century.

43 The parlour at Thornton Abbey was a finely proportioned but cold and cheerless room that implies necessity rather than sociability.

bay. On the floor were everyday objects: jet rosary beads, buttons, pens and *styli*, a wax tablet for writing on, two pewter plates, and coins, including a gold noble. Wall fireplaces indicate that this room had been used originally as the warming-house, the only room in the monastery apart from the kitchen where fires were allowed from November to Good Friday. Subsequently, it had been used as a day-room, for working and perhaps writing, judging from the finds it contained.

The side of the cloister opposite the church contained the refectory, a building whose importance in the daily life of the community was reflected by its scale and architectural pretensions (**44**). It was usually aligned parallel to the cloister alley, and might be at ground-floor level in Benedictine, Cluniac and Cistercian houses, though the canons and nuns of all orders preferred to have their refectory at first-floor level over a vaulted basement in emulation of the upper room in which Christ and the Disciples celebrated the Last Supper. From the mid twelfth century, the Cistercians adopted a different ground plan to other orders, placing the refectory at right angles to the cloister so that the kitchen which normally lay outside the range could be entered directly from the cloister alley. Whatever the planning, the arrangements of most refectories were the same, with a raised dais at the furthest end from the entrance where the president and

44 *At Fountains Abbey, the refectory survives to full height, though it has lost its central arcade. Around the walls, the raised foot-paces and the stubs of stone table legs can still be traced, whilst the wall pulpit occupied three bays of the west wall.*

senior officers of the convent sat, and raised foot-paces along the side walls on which benches and tables for the rest of the community were placed. Set in one wall towards the upper end of the room was a pulpit from which a member of the convent would read throughout meals, and close to the door from the cloister were cupboards set into the walls for napkins and spoons, as at Hailes, Haughmond and Kirkham. The body of the refectory was open space, so that the superior could observe all members of the community throughout the meal as St Benedict's rule required. Excavation of the fourteenth-century refectory of the Franciscan nuns at Denny Abbey revealed clearly how the refectory was organized, raised chalk foot-paces against the side walls, a dais at the east end for the Abbess, and an unbroken tiled floor throughout the central part of the building (45). An identical layout can be observed at Fountains Abbey where the bases of the stone table-legs remain in position, separated by shallow stair-cases through the raised foot-pace.

Attached to the refectory, but normally outside the cloister ranges and communicating by a hatch or short passage, was the kitchen, with its great fireplaces and ovens. True to the rule of St Benedict, the kitchen was for the preparation of a vegetarian diet. With the gradual adoption of meat into the monastic diet from the fourteenth century, a second meat kitchen was commonly provided, normally attached to the infirmary. Excavation of the kitchens at Kirkstall (see 55) and Sawley

Abbeys has revealed complex arrangements of drains that indicate the presence of piped water and the provision of sculleries. Sockets in the surviving masonry at Fountains Abbey evidence fitted cupboards or shelves. The plan of the kitchen was normally square, with a great louvred roof to take the smoke from a central hearth. In the greatest houses the kitchen was a substantial building like the great octagonal kitchen that survives at Durham or the abbot's kitchen at Glastonbury, with a vaulted roof that minimized the threat of fire.

The west range, which normally lay between the enclosed cloister and the semi-public Inner Court of the house provided the link between the religious and the outside world. In Cistercian houses it was the home of the laybrothers, the ground floor providing cellarage, an outer parlour and their refectory, the upper floor their dormitory. Other orders generally followed the pattern set by the Benedictines, with only the outer parlour and cellarage on the ground floor, and the president's lodging and perhaps guest accommodation above.

The west range of Monk Bretton Priory provides a well-preserved and perhaps typical model (46), surviving to a height of three floors and showing good evidence of continuing development from the thirteenth century. At ground-floor level and against the church was the outer parlour, covered with a barrel-vault, as dark and dismal as the canons' parlour in the east cloister range at Thornton. The central part of the range was simply a storehouse, initially vaulted, containing a well and having a mural stair to the first floor, whilst the southern bays were partitioned off to provide a service lobby that connected the kitchen and the foot of the

45 At Denny Abbey, excavation of the fourteenth-century refectory has revealed the tiled floor and foot-paces (J. Poster).

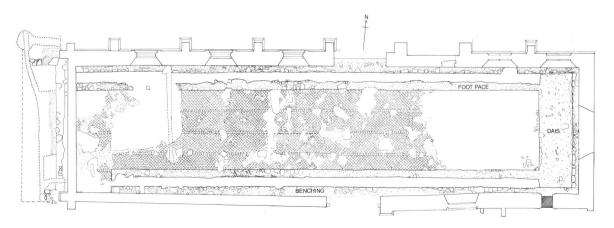

46 *The west range of Monk Bretton Priory comprised the prior's hall and chamber over an outer parlour and cellarage.*

stairs to the prior's lodging above.

At first-floor level, the same divisions of plan were maintained, with the southern bays forming the service end of the prior's hall and divided from it by a timber screen with a gallery above. His hall occupied the central part of the range and was provided with two broad windows of two lights, fitted with seats, in each side wall. It was heated by a central hearth carried on a pillar that still survives at ground level. The hall compares favourably with any of knightly class, serving to show the status of the prior within the house and his feudal rank in the outside world. It was a public room, where the most important visitors to the monastery were entertained or even lodged. The north end of the range comprised the prior's private chamber, a living and sleeping room originally divided from the hall by a timber partition. It was a room of the highest quality with an impressive fireplace and fine windows. On the west side, a door led to a timber-framed latrine tower, and a door in the north wall led to a private pew that looked down into a chapel in the south side of the church, a provision common to the powerful abbot of Westminster and the poor prioress of Wilberfoss. In the fifteenth century, the prior, not content with his substantial apartments, added a further heated room above his chamber, its south wall carried on a bold arch at the north end of his hall.

Infirmaries

Small monasteries often set apart one or more rooms in their cloister ranges as an infirmary for old and sick members of the community. In houses of middle or greater rank, however, separate accommodation was provided for those who could no longer endure the rigours of life in the cloister. Lying outside the cloister, and normally to the east of the east range away

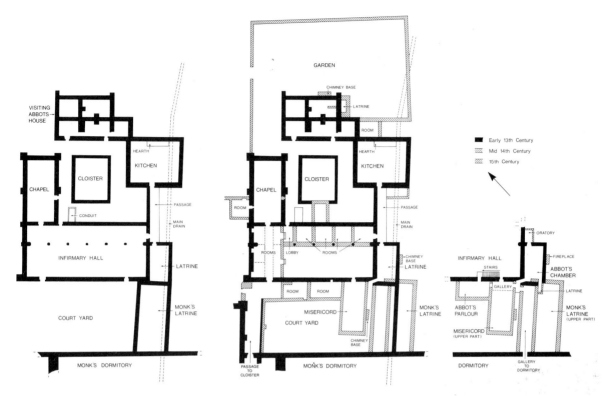

Early 13th Century
Mid 14th Century
15th Century

47 *The infirmary at Waverley Abbey (a) as it was built in the early years of the thirteenth century, (b) as it was modified in the fourteenth and fifteenth centuries, and (c) the possible layout of the fourteenth century abbot's house provided within the infirmary (after Brakspear).*

from the distractions of the Inner and Outer Courts, the infirmary duplicated many of the monastic buildings with its own hall, latrine, refectory, cloister and chapel. It often lay within its own enclosure, though it was entered from the main cloister. Fragments of many survive, as for instance at Christchurch Priory at Canterbury, or Gloucester, Peterborough, Rievaulx or Easby Abbeys. Others have been excavated to reveal their developing plan. Perhaps the most instructive of these is that built by the Cistercians at Waverley Abbey in the first years of the thirteenth century and excavated by Hope and the Rev. T. S. Cooper in 1899 (**47**).

Built early in the thirteenth century, the infirmary at Waverley replaced an earlier wooden building. It comprised a hall of six bays with a central hearth and a single aisle on its

east side, and a small cloister garth to the east. To the south of the infirmary hall and butting the monks' common latrine was a small latrine block associated with the infirmary. On the north side of the cloister lay the infirmary chapel, to the south its kitchen. Closing the east side was a domestic building of two storeys. In Cistercian monasteries this was the normal placing of a house for the abbot of the mother-house, who was obliged to visit annually to see that the daughter-house was being correctly run. In practice it tended to be used by abbots who had resigned, and the lower floor was used as the lodging of the infirmarer. The conduit from which water was piped to the main offices of the monastery was normally placed within the infirmary complex; at Waverley its base was found in the western alley of the infirmary cloister (see Chapter 4).

It is common to find radical changes in monastic infirmaries from the fourteenth century, and Waverley was no exception, with its buildings being extended and subdivided. The northernmost part of the hall was divided off and partitioned into at least five cubicles, each with its own fireplace, to give more privacy than the open ward of the old hall. Three rooms were built against the west wall in what had been an open court, the most southerly of which was the misericord or infirmary refectory, where meat could be eaten by not only the sick but also other members of the community, a sign that monastic life was becoming less austere. The availability of a meat diet drew senior members of the community to build their lodgings in the infirmary area, and at Waverley it was the abbot himself who moved his house there, using the misericord as his hall and having his meals prepared in the infirmary kitchen. The plan of his rather irregular lodging, untypical for a Cistercian abbot, can be recovered from the plan of the rooms below found in excavation. The fourteenth century also saw the enclosure of a garden to the east of the infirmary, a common feature on sites of every order.

The comfortable life available in the infirmary gradually became available to ordinary members of the community by the partitioning of the infirmary hall into private chambers. At Waverley this took place in the fifteenth century, at much the same time as the great infirmary hall at Fountains, one of the greatest aisled halls built in medieval England, was broken up into private apartments on two floors. Growing comfort can be demonstrated by the provision of more fireplaces. The great common ranges of the cloister had proved to be too cold and draughty, and shrinking communities were moving from them to the infirmary. At Byland Abbey, the old infirmary was demolished, its site occupied by individual two-room cells with wall-fireplaces, a certain sign that the idealistic communal life of the earlier Middle Ages was giving way to privacy and comfort for smaller groups of religious.

The Carthusian cloister

The Carthusians, who lived the life of hermits within their charterhouses, alone of English monks and nuns did not live a communal life. Instead, each monk occupied his own cell and garden, a personal monastery in miniature. Their buildings can best be seen at Mount Grace Priory, the best preserved of the English charterhouses, though excavation at Witham, Hinton and London has revealed similar arrangements. Set within a garden approximately 15.3 m (50 ft) square, each monk had a two-storey house. The ground floor comprised four rooms divided by timber partitions: an entry passage, a hall or living-room, a bed-room and oratory, and a study. The living-room had a fireplace and a stair leading to the upper floor, which comprised the work room, for every Carthusian was to have a trade. The garden was bounded by two corridors. One leading from the entry passage was a private cloister for study and meditation, and excavation has shown that these had windows with plain glass. The second corridor, entered from the living-room, was unglazed, and led to the garden and a latrine. A wall-niche in one of the two corridors contained a tap that supplied the cell with piped water.

The garden, which provided the monk with an opportunity for manual labour and a place for meditation, provided the only scope for personal expression in the most rigorous of monastic orders. Several of the Mount Grace gardens have been excavated, and no two are alike. That surrounding Cell 8 (**48**) was divided into rectangular beds defined by paths of roof-slate, the location of some of the individual plants being marked by slots or separate planting pits dug into the heavy clay subsoil and filled with richly-manured soil. In comparison, the garden of the adjacent Cell 9 had small square beds edged with stones in the manner of a knot garden. Such is the nature of the subsoil at Mount Grace that little evidence of plant seeds or pollen has survived to be identified.

Gardens

Monastic gardens were common. They can be traced in frequent references in suppression period surveys and have a long history going back to the ninth century plan of St Gall. At Wilberfoss Priory, the 1535 survey concludes: 'Item ane orchard where the dovecote standyth, ane acre di., fulle of esh trees. Item gardyns.' At Rievaulx two gardens are mentioned: the abbot's garden, and the kitchen garden, as well as the cloister garth which must have been gardened in some way. Gardens were normally enclosed and provided a spiritual metaphor. The garden of the Song of Solomon symbolized a virgin bride; by extension in the monastic world it symbolized the Virgin Mary as well as providing an earthly paradise for the community. At Christchurch Cathedral priory in Canterbury, the layout of the late-twelfth-century infirmary cloister garden is known from the contemporary drawing of the monastic

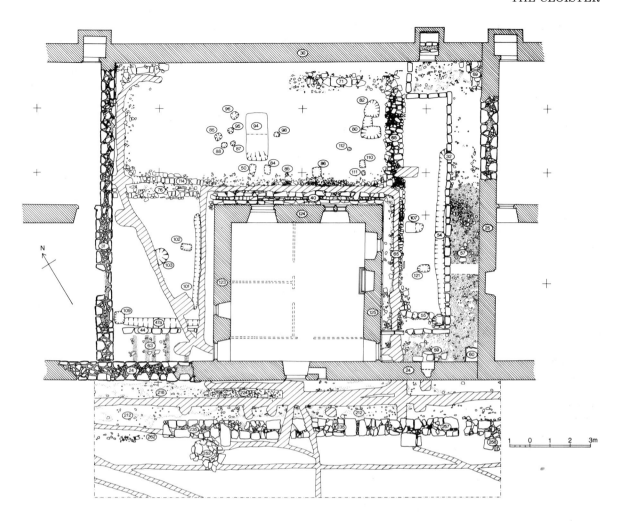

48 *Excavation of Cell 8 at Mount Grace Priory has revealed the paths, planting pits, and cultivation of trenches of a late-medieval garden (D. Coppack).*

waterworks. Labelled the *herbarium*, the enclosure is shown with rows of plants and wooden trellises.

The plants grown in English *herbaria* can perhaps be identified with the contemporary herbals that were found in monastic libraries from as far back as the early twelfth century. Archaeology, however, is at last giving an insight into monastic gardening, though very few gardens have been excavated, largely because past emphasis has been on the study of cloister buildings. One of the first to have been examined, though the results were very disappointing, was the cloister garden at Denny

Abbey. Though no trace of bedding trenches were found or plant remains identified, the garden soil was found to have been highly cultivated and full of the remains of domestic refuse dug in as fertilizer. At the centre was a cistern, presumably to provide a source for watering the plants. More instructive was the garden of the Augustinian friary at Hull, where deep trenches had been dug into the heavy clay subsoil and filled with compost and domestic refuse. Waterlogging ensured the survival of seeds and pollens to allow the eventual identification of the species grown. The layout of the bedding trenches (**49**) shows that the garden was of formal design. More recently, the cloister garth of the Gilbertine house at York has been excavated, with bedding trenches for box hedges dividing formal plots within the garth, extending the formality of the cloister arcades

79

to the centre of the enclosure. In 1444, Brother Thomas Suthewelle of Bardney Abbey was criticized by the sacrist for building a garden in the cloister there during the bishop's visitation of the house. This would suggest that there had previously been no garden there but that the garth was grassed. His garden remains to be excavated, and the cause of the sacrist's displeasure disclosed. Our conception of monastic ruins with neatly lawned cloisters may well have seemed strange to the religious who occupied those buildings when they were a living community.

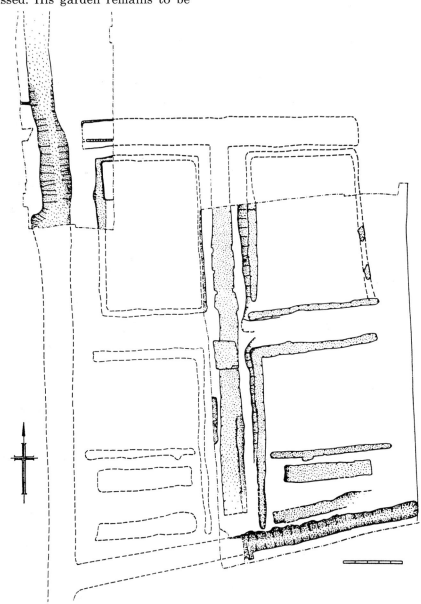

49 *A more formal monastic layout can be seen in the garden of the Augustinian friary in Hull, where substantial trenches filled with well-manured soil were dug into the sterile clay and show the pattern of planting (Humberside Archaeological Unit).*

1. The gatehouse and western part of the precinct at Thornholme Priory as they would have appeared in the middle years of the fourteenth century (Judith Dobie).

2. A late twelfth century copy of the charter by which Walter Espec gave his new Cistercian foundation of Rievaulx lands in Ryedale and Bilsdale in 1145, preserved in the abbey's collected charters or cartulary, a book in the collection of Sir Robert Cotton (British Library).

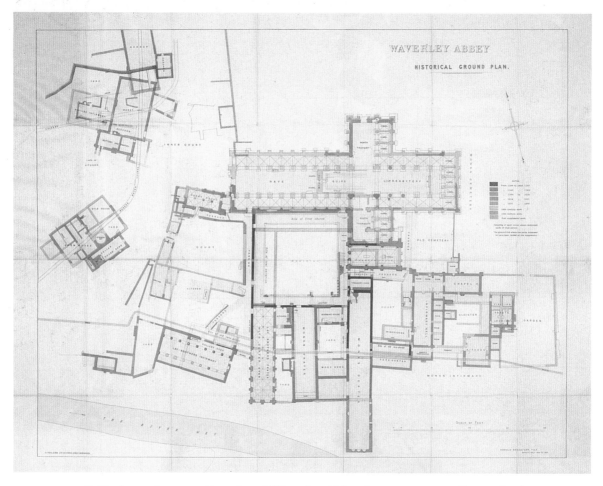

3. Brakspear's excavation plan of Waverley Abbey in contrast to earlier work shows the phasing of the buildings in great detail.

4. Fountains Abbey provided a vista for John Aislabie's water gardens at Studley Royal, seen in this painting of about 1760 across the Half Moon Pond (National Trust).

5. Kirkstall Abbey, as drawn by William Richardson in the 1840s, was still a Romantic ruin in open country, though this was not to last as Leeds spread westwards.

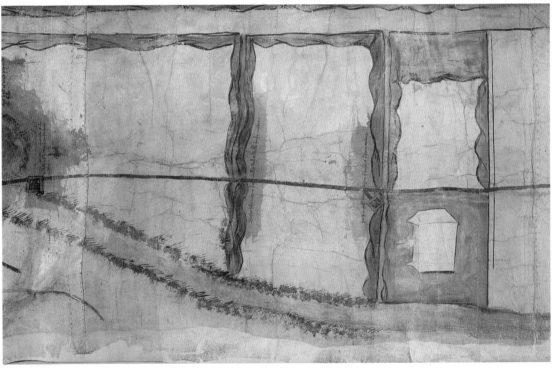

6. The London Carthusian charterhouse installed a piped water supply from Islington in 1430, recorded on a detailed map. This map was altered on several occasions by the convent's plumber, showing how the system had been improved up to 1512 (English Heritage).

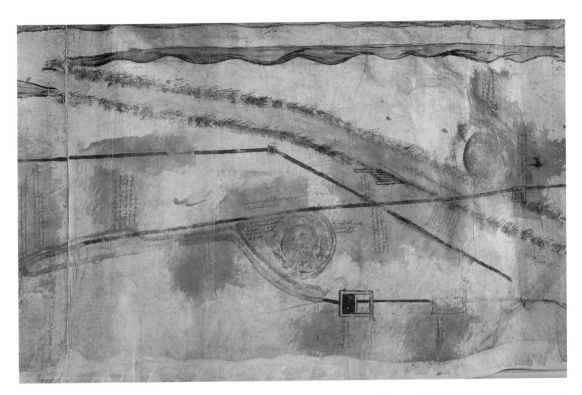

7. 'Robin Hood's Well' at
Fountains Abbey, one of the
well-houses that supplied
piped water to the cloister
ranges from the 1160s
(author).

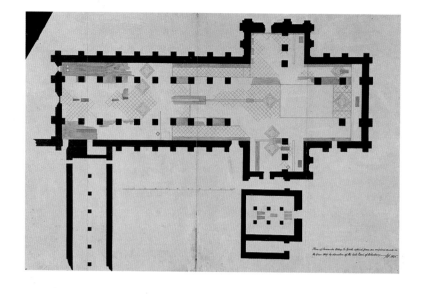

8. John Claridge's plan of the
church, chapter-house, and
west range at Jervaulx
survives as a copy of 1845
(Yorkshire Museum).

9. The chapter-house at Jervaulx, once cleared of debris, became an open promenade within a Romantic landscape, its architectural detail set off against trees and shrubs that still give the site its special character today (William Richardson).

10. The Pershore barn at Leigh Court, built in the vernacular tradition of the west of England, would indicate that the Cistercians were not alone in the building of great barns on their granges (English Heritage).

11. The nave of Byland Abbey as it was built in the late twelfth and early
thirteenth centuries (Simon Hayfield).

4

Sanitation

One of the most remarkable aspects of monastic life was the pre-occupation with the provision of a plentiful water supply, not only for drinking and washing, but also to flush drains, fill fish-ponds and service the buildings of the Outer Court. Two separate supplies were needed, for potable water and water used to flush the drains were never mixed except as waste. The vast quantities of water required by even a small monastery was an important factor in the initial siting of a house, and the failure of an expected supply might indeed cause the abandonment of a site. The Augustinian priory of Wigmore in Herefordshire was first established at Shobdon, but moved to a place called Eye near Aymestrey because the canons found that they were 'too far from the water they sorely lacked'. Their patron insisted that they abandon that site in favour of a site adjacent to the church at Wigmore, where again they found the site 'above all . . . very short of water' and moved again to a more suitable site to the north of the village.

Ideally, a monastery would be placed on a river, as at Fountains, Roche or Waverley, and the river water made to work for the house. This was not always possible, particularly for urban houses, and an alternative supply had to be engineered, often at great expense and with remarkable ingenuity. Great vaulted drains flushed by distant watercourses were built to serve latrines, rivers were diverted or leats canalized to serve the mills and industrial buildings of the precinct, and drinking water was brought from wells or springs and piped throughout the major buildings of the monastery. Even engineered supplies could not be guaranteed, as the monks of Waverley discovered in 1215. The aqueduct that brought water from the spring of *Ludwelle* 'not without astonishment dried up', and it was only after

'great difficulty, enquiring, and invention, and not without much labour and sweating' that Symon, one of the monks, located a new spring some 480 m (1560 ft) to the east of the abbey buildings and brought its waters to the house by underground conduits.

Excavation and ground survey has demonstrated that such major undertakings were not restricted to the wealthiest houses but even poor nuns and friars could expect a clean water supply and efficient drains. Because clean water and good sanitation were a necessity of monastic life the majority of religious houses were provided with both at a time when the only other buildings to enjoy these luxuries were royal and episcopal palaces. It is only the scale and complexity of hydraulic engineering that varies from house to house. Because these provisions were central to monastic life they tended to date from the earliest years of development, though they would undoubtedly be modified as the needs of the establishment changed.

Monastic plumbing and medieval documents

The starting point for the archaeological study of the monastic water supply is the surviving collection of medieval drawings that show how water was supplied. Of these, the most useful are two late-twelfth-century drawings, which show in remarkable detail how water was brought to the great cathedral priory of Christchurch in Canterbury, and a much amended waterworks plan of the early fifteenth century from the Carthusian charterhouse of London. The Canterbury drawings can be dated from associated documents to the priorate of Wybert, 1153–67, and show in great detail the total water system for the house.

Christchurch had begun its life at the very

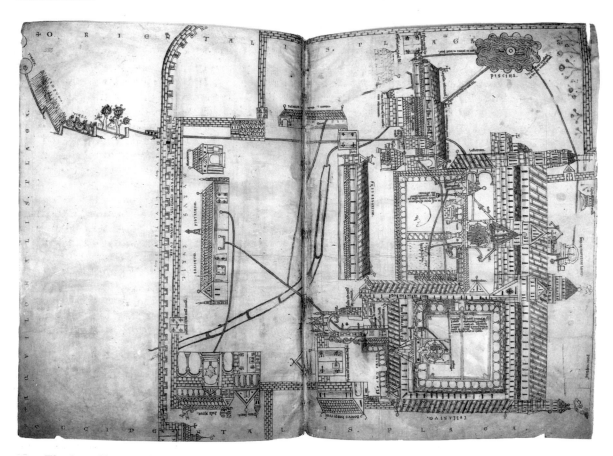

50 *The installation of a piped water supply at Canterbury was recorded in remarkable detail on an accurate drawing of the house, showing not only the pipe-runs but even the architectural detail of the monastic buildings (Trinity College, Cambridge).*

end of the sixth century on a site within the Roman city without ready access to water. The Saxon monastery, and its successor built by Archbishop Lanfranc after a fire in 1067, had relied on wells, and it was only the granting of a source of spring water 1.2 km (¾ mile) to the north-east of the city by Archbishop Theobald, or more likely St Thomas Becket, that guaranteed a sufficient supply for a convent of perhaps 200 monks. The first drawing shows the mechanics of bringing water from the source, a large spring-fed pond. The water was collected in a conduit house or tower and brought along the line of the present Military Road in a pipe, past a cultivated field, a vineyard and an orchard. Five settling tanks were provided to filter the water, the supply pipe entering at the

base and leaving at the top of each tank. Each settling tank also had a drain-cock for servicing it. Remarkably, this system, protected by an Act of Parliament in 1545, is still running. The supply pipe was brought across the town ditch, through the defensive wall, and into the precinct. From there its course is better followed on the second plan (**50**), shown in blue. It ran first to a great laver in the infirmary cloister, passing a well which was perhaps an earlier source. From here water was led to the laver outside the refectory door in the great cloister. Both of these lavers were of considerable architectural sophistication. The colour-coding of the plan changes from blue to red once water has left these two great *lavatoria*, showing that they were primary sources with the cleanest water. Here perhaps is a clue to the importance of the monastic water supply, for these two lavers have an undoubted spiritual significance that required copious supplies of the purest water. From the laver in the great cloister, water was distributed throughout the priory, with a pipe carried below the refectory to the kitchen, from which a pipe was led to the brewhouse and bakehouse. A branch off this fed a building labelled 'bath-house and chamber', and from the kitchen a further supply was taken to the guest hall, the *Aula Nova*, where there was another monumental laver. A second feed from the laver in the great cloister led to the infirmary, where there was yet another laver or fountain from which a supply was taken to the prior's chambers. From this main supply, a branch-pipe led below the church to feed a fountain in the great lay cemetery, alongside which was a well, presumably part of the earlier supply system. Once water had been distributed to all the major buildings of the house, the waste was used to feed a great and decorative fish-pond in the Court, and was then channelled back to flush the infirmary latrine and the great latrine block attached to the monks' dormitory. From there, waste was flushed across the Outer Court in a vaulted drain which debouched well away from the priory buildings into the town ditch. Surface water from the great cloister and the church roofs was also used to help flush this sewer, in stone channels, coloured yellow.

The scale and sophistication of Prior Wybert's supply is immediately apparent from the two drawings, but many details are lacking. Only excavation can confirm if the pipes are of wood or lead, or how the system was later modified as buildings were replaced or remodelled. Although many taps or cocks are shown on the second drawing, none survives to show their form, and all the great lavers have been destroyed. It is also not certain whether Wybert's system was the first to be installed or whether he had added a permanent supply to an existing layout.

In comparison, the London plan, one of two near-identical plots, tells us a great deal more. Drawn up when the house was first given its own permanent water source at Islington in 1430, 61 years after its foundation, and altered at least twice before 1512, it is very much a working drawing for the convent's plumbers (**colour plate 6**). Deletions and insertions in the manuscript show how the system was adapted and how exactly the water was collected, filtered and directed. Originally four springs were enclosed, linked by a stone gutter, but by 1512 two more enclosed springs and two open springs had been added to the system. From the closest spring to the house, around

1.5 km (1 mile) to the south, a lead pipe carried all the collected water to a conduit house, the White Conduit, which survived as remodelled by Thomas Sutton as late as 1831 in Denmark Road, Islington. Two pipes led from the conduit: a waste pipe carrying off any surplus, and the 'home pipe'. The home pipe ran through a series of settling tanks, described on the plot as 'wells', first as a single feed, then doubled, and finally trebled, to a second conduit house shown in elevation on the plan. To prevent the pressure of water breaking the pipe, a series of vents or 'suspirels' were provided, and these also acted as drain-cocks for cleansing the pipe. From the second conduit an enlarged home pipe ran directly to the house, skirting two mill-mounds and passing below the highway from Islington to London where the pipe 'goth in a pece of oke kev(er)ed w^t a creste of oke ovyr the diche'. Running with the home pipe are the water supplies of the Clerkenwell nuns and the great hospital-priory of St John of Clerkenwell, over whose lands the charterhouse pipe passed by licence. The home pipe ran to the centre of the great cloister of the charterhouse, feeding a lead cistern in a fine octagonal conduit house or 'age', from which water was led in pipes to each of the monks' cells, the cloister laver and the buildings of the Inner Court. Finally the pipe passed out of the precinct to supply a convent building called 'Egipt', and the 'Wyndmyll', the 'Elmys', and the 'Hertis horne', taverns that enjoyed the waste water with the permission of the convent.

Water sources

Monastic water supplies were often retained after the dissolution to serve new mansions surviving well into the post-medieval period. Remarkably little attention has ever been paid to them, and only one source has ever been examined archaeologically, though others are known. Recent excavations at Canterbury have revealed the spring-house that supplied the great Benedictine abbey of St Augustine from the twelfth century (**51**). Lying just to the east of the source used by Christchurch cathedral priory a series of springs fed an open pond. Early in the thirteenth century, the pond was replaced by a polygonal tank of flint and Caen stone dug into the hillside on the spring-line. This tank was fed by no less than 25 separate springs, each of them tapped by a vaulted addit or stone-lined channel, and, where examination

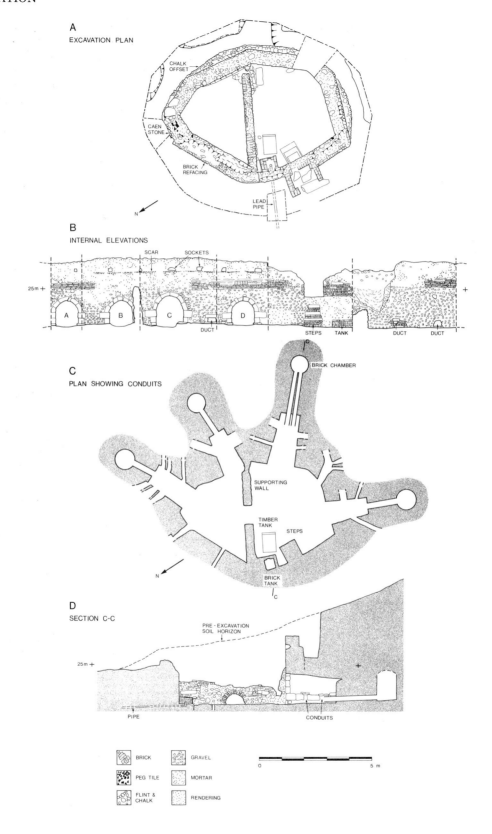

A
EXCAVATION PLAN

CHALK
OFFSET

CAEN
STONE

BRICK
REFACING

LEAD
PIPE

N

B
INTERNAL ELEVATIONS

SCAR   SOCKETS

25m

A   B   C   D

DUCT   STEPS   TANK   DUCT   DUCT

C
PLAN SHOWING CONDUITS

BRICK CHAMBER

SUPPORTING
WALL

TIMBER
TANK   STEPS

N

BRICK
TANK

C

D
SECTION C-C

PRE-EXCAVATION
SOIL HORIZON

25m

PIPE   CONDUITS

BRICK   GRAVEL

PEG TILE   MORTAR

FLINT &   RENDERING
CHALK

0   5 m

51 *Excavation to permit conservation of its remains has revealed the details of the spring-house that served St Augustine's Abbey in Canterbury from the early thirteenth century up to the present day (after Canterbury Archaeological Trust).*

was possible, the springs themselves rose within little vaulted chambers. This source survived the destruction of St Augustine's Abbey in 1540, being retained to serve the palace that Henry VIII established there, and it was repaired and refitted in the later seventeenth century. This work unfortunately removed any evidence of how water was led from the spring-house originally. The tank was also reroofed in the seventeenth century, and no trace remained of how it was covered in the Middle Ages, though it must have been totally enclosed to ensure an uncontaminated supply.

In comparison, individual well or spring-houses are more common survivors. One of the earliest (**colour plate 7**) can still be seen at Fountains Abbey, known since the Middle Ages as 'Robin Hood's Well'. Built in the 1160s, it was fed by an open conduit that can still be traced on the ground from a large open tank in the south-east corner of the precinct, an engineered replacement for one of the natural springs that gave the abbey its name. From it, water was piped to a distribution point in the infirmary, serving the eastern part of the abbey. A second supply was provided by another open tank in the south-western part of the precinct, and pipes running from it have been seen below the wool-house in the Outer Court, leading water towards the laybrothers' infirmary where there must have been a second conduit house. The piping of water first to the infirmaries at Fountains is strangely reminiscent of Prior Wybert's supply at Canterbury, and the further identification of conduit houses attached to the infirmary at Waverley (see **47**) and Beaulieu revealed in excavations of the early 1900s might suggest that this was the normal course of events.

52 *Two of the three well-houses that supplied drinking water at Mount Grace Priory reconstructed after excavation in the 1960s.*

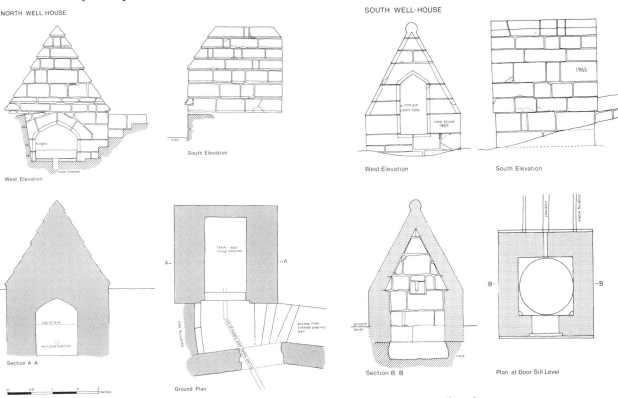

NORTH WELL HOUSE

South Elevation

West Elevation

Section A-A

Ground Plan

SOUTH WELL-HOUSE

West Elevation

South Elevation

Section B-B

Plan at Door Sill Level

Similar provision was made for the Carthusians at Mount Grace. Like their brothers of London they enjoyed a piped supply to each of their cells, but they did not have to go so far to find a supply. Three natural springs on the hillside immediately above the site were tapped, each with its own little well-house (**52**). Two were excavated in the 1960s during the general clearance of the site and were found to have been thrown down by robbers who removed the valuable lead tanks and pipework, and were reconstructed with some additional stonework. The spring that supplied the house with drinking water lay to the north-east of the priory. It contained a tank 1.5 m (5 ft) long, 0.9 m (3 ft) wide and 0.6 m (2 ft) deep, and from this a lead supply pipe carefully laid in a pear-sectioned channel between two layers of stone flags was taken below ground to a conduit-house at the centre of the great cloister, very much on the model of the London charterhouse. Where it passed through the outer wall of the east range there must have been a cock to draw off surplus water that was channelled away in a surviving drain to flush the foul sewers. Where the supply pipe passed within the monastery, it was enclosed within a sectional ashlar channel of interlocking sections. The feed depended on gravity, just as it did at Canterbury and Fountains, and there was no evidence of pumping. Even with a gravity feed from just above the site pressure in the pipes seems to have been a problem and 'suspirels' of a similar form to those shown on the London plan can be identified at Mount Grace.

The cloister laver

Several attempts have been made to identify and date the provision of piped water to claustral ranges by excavation. One of the earliest was the excavation of the laver in the great cloister at Durham by Hope in 1903. Like the monks at Christchurch, the Benedictines at Durham had a piped supply that fed amongst other offices:

'within ye cloyster garth over against ye fraterhouse dour . . . a fair laver or counditt for ye mouncks to washe ther handes & faces at, being made in forme Round covered with lead and all of marble saving ye verie uttermost walls. Wthin ye wch walls yow may walke rownd about ye laver of marble having many litle Cunditts or spouts of brasse wth xxiiij

Cockes of brasse Rownd about yt, havinge in yt vij faire wyndowes of stone woorke, and in the Top of yt a faire dovecotte, covered over about wth lead . . .'.

The 1903 excavation set a very high standard for its day, with the examination of the whole structure to reveal a series of building phases. Hope resolved the sequence logically with reference to the exceptional documentary evidence available for Durham, and so meticulous was his reporting that the site is still capable of reinterpretation (**53**).

The earliest laver, dated by its recovered architectural components to the late twelfth century, lay in the south-west corner of the first cloister garth, and comprised a circular structure 2.5 m (8 ft) in diameter set within a square enclosure, apparently the base for an open arcade. This was clearly secondary to the main cloister arcade, the plinth wall of which had been cut back when the laver was built. The circular base of the laver, sections of which had been reused in later work, was decorated with an arcade of 15 blind arches and had supported a basin that was not recovered. At its centre, a lead pipe rose up from a stone-lined channel to feed the basin much in the manner of the Canterbury drawing. The pipe itself was traced for some 12.5 m (41 ft) towards the centre of the cloister where it terminated against a stone base, and a second channel ran off to the west from the same point. The water pipe was turned upwards against the base, and 1.5 m (5 ft) to the east was a stone-lined well which had every appearance of being twelfth century in date. Hope drew the obvious parallel of the well and 'pillar' adjacent to the laver in the infirmary cloister at Christchurch, Canterbury, which was captioned 'Pillar into which, when the water supply fails, water from the well can be poured and will be supplied to all the offices'. At Durham, this appears to have been the original arrangement.

Early in the thirteenth century, the great cloister was extended to the west and the old laver and its enclosure demolished. It was replaced on the same site by the octagonal buttressed structure so graphically described in the late-sixteenth-century source quoted above. This rebuilding coincided with the provision of an engineered water supply brought from outside the precinct to the south, and the supply from the old well was redirected towards

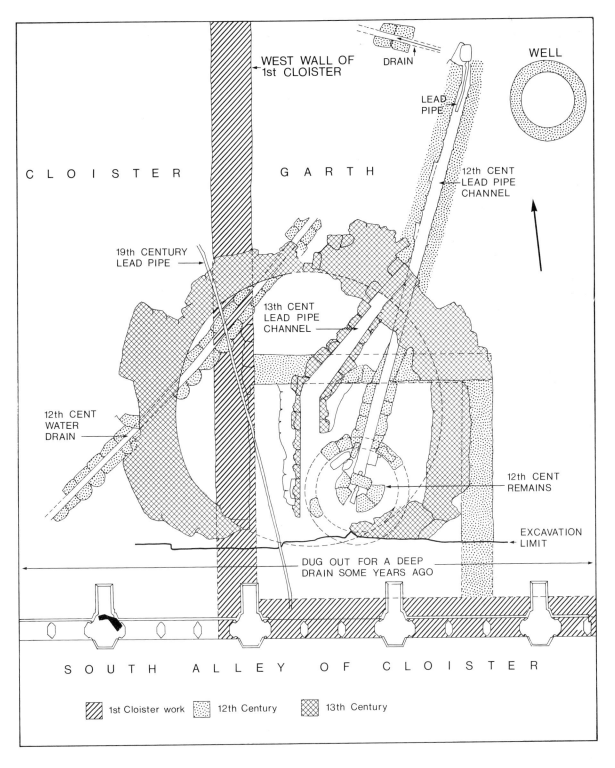

53 *The excavation of the cloister laver at Durham in 1903 revealed two major phases of construction, reinterpreted from the original drawings of Charles Hodgson Fowler.*

the centre of the new structure, though the main supply came from a pipe laid in a stone channel that ran from below the refectory to meet the well supply. Both branches of the new channel were lined with sections of the old circular laver, demonstrating their contemporaneity. No trace of the laver that occupied the octagonal structure survived. From the bursar's accounts of 1338–9 and the following year, it is clear that a fully engineered supply could not always be guaranteed: 'to women

54 *A reconstruction of the fifteenth-century laver basin at Durham based on its surviving elements.*

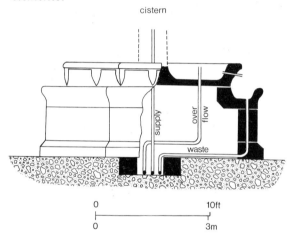

56 *(Right.) Clean water was distributed at Kirkstall from a series of cisterns, originally lined with lead and acting additionally as filters (after Wrathmell and Moorhouse).*

carrying water from the Wear to the abbey for the bakehouse, brewhouse, and kitchen at divers times when the pipe was frozen' and 'in drawing water from the draw-well in the cloister and for work about the pipe'.

A third phase in the development of the laver is apparent from the surviving laver basin now lying at the centre of the great cloister (**54**) which can be identified as the laver of the sixteenth century description. An octagonal pedestal is drilled to take a rising pipe that fed a fountain at the centre of the basin, and water was drawn off from the basin through 12 pipes with double taps (the 'xxiiij Cockes of brasse') to feed a lower trough. The level of water in the basin was controlled by an overflow pipe, and the fountain must have run continually. All the plumbing was evidenced by pipe-holes drilled in the marble. According to contemporary accounts, this new laver was provided in

55 *Excavation at Kirkstall Abbey in the 1950s recovered considerable evidence for the development of water supply and drainage (after Wrathmell and Moorhouse).*

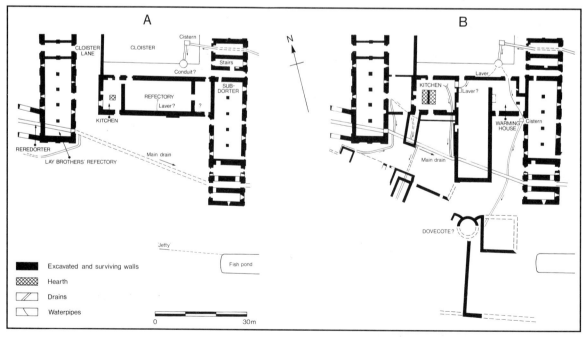

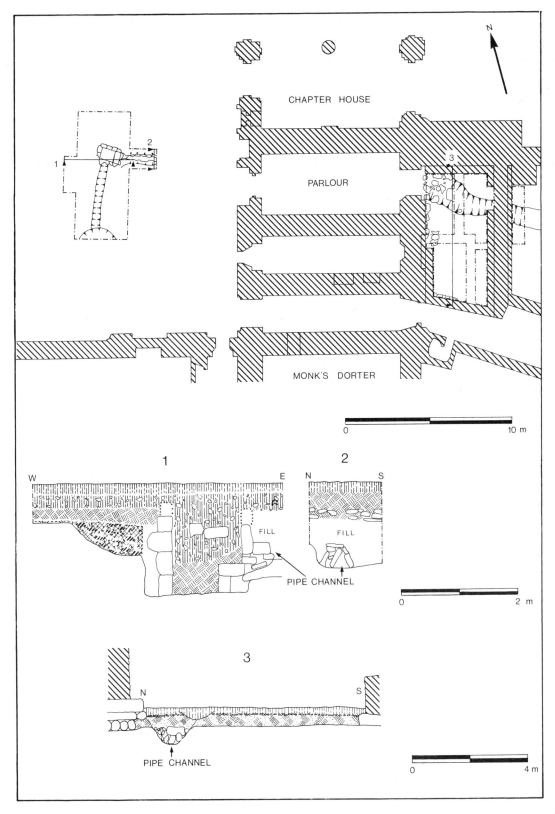

CHAPTER HOUSE

PARLOUR

MONK'S DORTER

0   10 m

1

W   E

FILL

PIPE CHANNEL

2

N   S

FILL

0   2 m

3

N   S

PIPE CHANNEL

0   4 m

1432–3, the year in which the single stone of the basin and the two stones of the trough were quarried at Eggleston.

The archaeology of water systems

More recently, excavations at Kirkstall Abbey in the 1950s, recently reconsidered, recovered good evidence of a developing water system of which the earliest phase was contemporary with the earliest stone buildings on site, that is, the early 1160s (55). The Cistercians, with their fundamentalist interpretation of the Benedictine rule, might be expected to have provided only water that was strictly necessary for liturgical and social needs, and this seems to be confirmed by the evidence of excavation. Not all the pipe runs were identified by the original excavators as robbing of the lead had confused the situation. In spite of this, enough was recovered to show how the supply was developed. The earliest supply was located below the parlour in the east cloister range, a robbed pipe originally protected by a conduit of pitched stones coming from the general area of the infirmary to feed a cistern in the southeast corner of the great cloister, passing through and contemporary with the footings of the east range. The cistern (56) was lined with cut stone, with a step on its east side below which the pipe entered. It must originally have been lined with lead if it was to hold water, but any lining had been removed at the suppression together with the pipes. The cistern appears to have acted as a filter as an outlet in its south side was approximately 30 cm (1 ft) higher than the inlet, and this led to a circular robber pit on the line of the south cloister arcade. Was this the site of a detached laver similar to that found by Hope at Durham and so favoured by the early Cistercians in France? Sadly, excavation was incomplete in this area, though future work might resolve the problem. Waste water was carried away from this feature to the south in a drain below the south cloister range, where it ran into the main monastic sewer to help flush the monks' latrines. This drain was later removed, its robber trench carefully packed with pitched rubble to prevent subsidence. Further pipe runs of the first building period were not identified, but a section of lead pipe traced only by its clay packing was found running from the south wall of the original east-west refectory to the centre of the room where it appeared to terminate in a small

laver and must have been fed from somewhere. Only re-excavation will resolve the true nature of the primary plumbing at Kirkstall.

The initial layout was extended from the last quarter of the twelfth century (55) when the east-west refectory was rebuilt on a north-south axis and the new building provided with a *lavatorium* set in the south wall of the adjacent cloister alley. Unfortunately, the link between the old and new lavers was not examined archaeologically, but further sections of pipework were discovered. This additional pipework was not protected by stone channels or clay packing, but was set in deep and irregular trenches. A supply was brought from the west range to a scullery to the south of the kitchen, and a pipe was run from the old laver in the cloister, through the warming-room, to a stone-lined cistern in the yard to the south. Like its predecessor in the great cloister it must originally have had a lead lining. From here a water supply was taken south, not in a pipe but a stone culvert, below the monastic sewer to unexcavated buildings in the Inner Court. A small laver against the west wall of the refectory was fed by a pipe which led from the new *lavatorium* in the south wall of the cloister. One of the most obvious effects of supplying water to the cloister ranges is that once used it had to be disposed of. Stone-built drains were therefore provided to carry away waste water from the kitchen and scullery, and from the west range, discharging into the main sewer.

Few if any piped water supplies can be dated before the middle years of the twelfth century, and it would appear that either the technology required had not been developed sufficiently or the lead itself was not available in large enough quantities to permit its widespread use. The latter is most likely, for it is not until the final quarter of the century that lead was regularly used for roofing. Indeed, it was not until 1179–84 that the tile roofs of the great abbey church of Waltham in Essex were replaced by 290 cart-loads of lead brought from Yorkshire and Derbyshire 'for the work of the church'.

The technology of pipe manufacture was borrowed from the Roman plumbers of 12 centuries earlier, and seems to have appeared fully developed in England, changing little throughout the Middle Ages. The technique of manufacture has recently been defined following the examination of excavated pipes. The pipes themselves were made in sections of

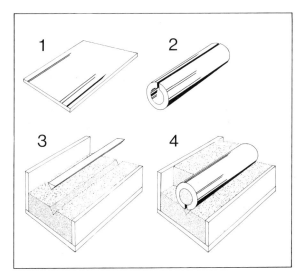

57 *The method of making lead water pipes was developed from that first introduced to Britain by the Romans, using simple but effective technology.*

roughly 3 m (10 ft) in length and of varying internal diameters ranging from as little as 2.5 cm (1 in.) to more than 10 cm (4 in.). These lengths were then joined by collars (**57**). Each section was cut from cast lead sheet and formed around a wooden mandrel to leave an open seam on its upper surface. The mandrel was then withdrawn and the pipe filled with casting sand. The next operation took place on the casting table, a large tray of damp sand, when a wooden template was used to form a triangular depression over which the open seam of the pipe was placed. Molten lead was then run into the depression to seal the open seam and leave a distinctive ridge on the upper surface of the pipe. Once the pipe had cooled, it was removed from the casting table, cleaned up, and joined to other sections by soldering on the previously-cast jointing collars. Any bending of a pipe section had to be done before the casting sand was removed, and the plumbers' workshop would need to be fairly close to the final location of the pipework. The collars were the weak part of the system and most likely to leak, and consequently it is common to find pipe-runs laid in a bed of puddled clay, in either a stone-lined channel or an earth-dug trench, to prevent leakage.

Water supplies did not consist simply of pipes, and archaeology has provided evidence of sophisticated filtering systems. In some cases, this comprised a tank fitted with a pierced grille that removed the most obvious impurities, and pierced lead filter plates are a common find on monastic sites. More sophisticated methods were also used. An early discovery in the south cloister range at Westminster Abbey comprised a lead cistern set within a stone-built cupboard in the side wall of a service passage. All the lead-work had

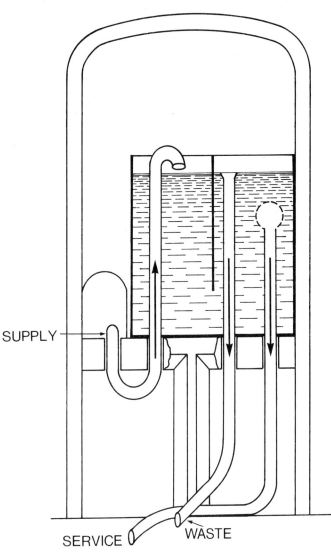

58 *Cleanliness required water to be filtered as it passed around the system, achieved by the use of filters and settling tanks such as this example from the south cloister range of Westminster Abbey (after Micklethwaite).*

been stripped out in the sixteenth century when the building was derelict, but a study of the surviving pipe holes cut in the stonework and excavation of the debris lying on the passage floor recovered enough information to reconstruct the original arrangements (58). A lead tank, apparently supported by an internal wooden frame, was placed on a stone shelf within the niche with three pipes entering through its base, one a feed from the source, one the service pipe that ran to a tap fed from the cistern, and the third an overflow pipe that returned surplus water to the rest of the system. Impurities would fall as sediment to the bottom of the tank and could be cleaned out periodically. A fine lead grille found in the debris on the passage floor was thought to have covered the mouth of the service pipe to prevent any floating debris getting as far as the tap. As the wall it was set in dated to the late fourteenth century, the filter arrangement cannot date from any earlier. A simpler arrangement was found in the east guest-house at Fountains Abbey amongst sixteenth-century demolition debris thrown into a latrine shaft. Almost certainly it had come from the upper floor of the guest house and comprised the lead lining

of a wooden tank and two sections of fitting pipe of differing internal diameters, both of which had been cut off to salvage the greater lengths of pipe.

Taps

Allied to the technology of the pipework was the provision of taps. The Durham laver with its 24 brass taps was not particularly unusual, and cloister *lavatoria* were provided with cast taps of brass or latten from the third quarter of the twelfth century. Remarkably, a number of taps have survived, recovered by excavation (59). Richard Walbran's excavation of Fountains in the 1850s produced a two-piece tap which appears to be associated with the cloister laver of *c.* 1170. From the 1950s excavations at nearby Kirkstall came two further tap-keys of the later twelfth century, again stylistically contemporary with the cloister lavatory from which it was assumed they were derived. As both these taps came from later medieval or suppression period contexts it can be assumed that they had survived in use to the last years of monastic life. A further late-twelfth-century tap was recovered from Kilburn Priory in the late nineteenth century. Later taps include a

A

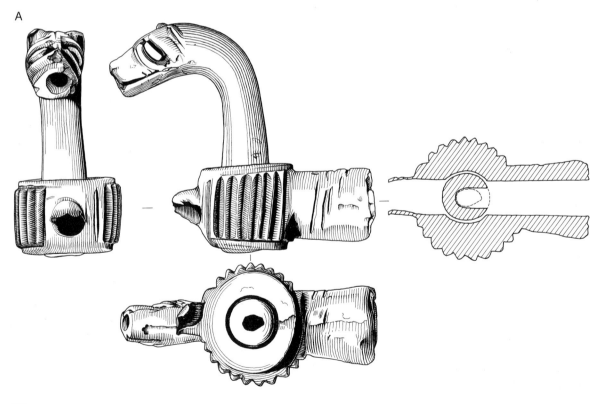

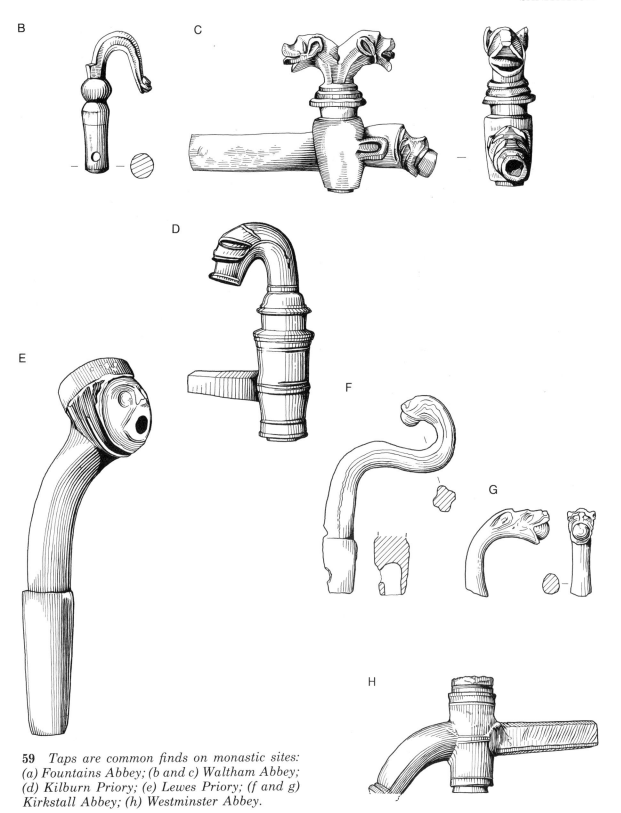

59 *Taps are common finds on monastic sites:*
(a) Fountains Abbey; (b and c) Waltham Abbey;
(d) Kilburn Priory; (e) Lewes Priory; (f and g)
Kirkstall Abbey; (h) Westminster Abbey.

tap-key from Lewes, found with a group of scrap metal apparently looted from the great Cluniac priory there, and dated by the costume of the woman depicted on it to the early years of the thirteenth century; a complete tap and a tap-key from late medieval and later deposits at Waltham Abbey; and a tap from Westminster Abbey associated with the water filter described above, perhaps as late as the fourteenth century. Whilst some taps were undoubtedly fixed directly to a pipe, there is a growing body of evidence to show that many were fed from a tank or open trough or basin similar to those of the Durham or Canterbury lavers. Recent re-examination of the marble cloister laver trough from Byland Abbey has revealed that it is not in fact a trough at all but a reservoir, originally lined with lead, its front face drilled with a series of holes that carried short lengths of pipe feeding a whole series of taps. A metal trough below comprised the actual washing-place (**60**), a similar arrangement to that evidenced in the surviving *lavatoria* at Fountains and Rievaulx. Indeed, the basin at Rievaulx was described in 1538 as being of lead overlaid with pewter, though fragments of a marble tank do survive.

Ceramic and wooden pipes
Although the use of lead for pipes is almost universal, alternative materials were used and have been identified by excavation. The most common alternative was ceramic sectional pipes. Excavation on the north side of the church at Kirkham Priory in 1978 revealed a pottery water-pipe carefully laid in puddled clay and sealed by the second structural phase of the church, dated by its architectural detail to 1160–70. Only a short length of the pipe lay within the area under excavation, but seven near-identical pipe sections were recovered (**61**). The pipe passed below the church towards the cloister laver, and was large enough to comprise a major, if not the principal, supply, for it traversed the hillside on which the priory was built from the spring-line above. Supply pipes to the laver itself and to other cloister buildings were of lead as is evidenced by the size of holes cut in the masonry to take them, and it would seem that Kirkham had a mixed system. Smaller pottery pipes are known from Thetford Priory, where they appear to have acted as both supply pipes and waste drains, and from the Lincoln Greyfriars, where they have been interpreted as a supply pipe from the conduit head.

Far less common are wooden pipes, for unless they were jointed with iron collars they are unlikely to survive on most sites and are difficult to identify in excavation. Rare examples are known from Beaulieu Abbey, where they were used to take water to the house from its distant conduit, the woolhouse at Fountains Abbey, where a section of wooden pipe had been reused as a drain, its open end closed with a lead cap, and at Thornholme Priory, where a

60 *The form of the Byland Abbey laver, with its marble tank and metal trough can be reconstructed from fragments recovered by excavation (after Harrison).*

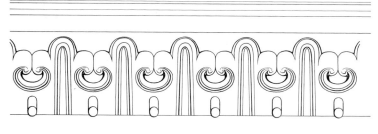

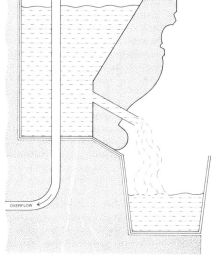

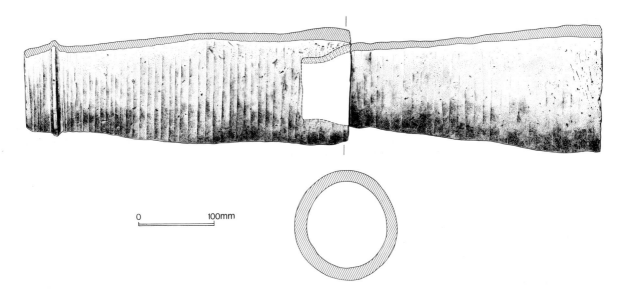

61 *Pottery water pipes from Kirkham Priory, dating from the third quarter of the twelfth century.*

fragment of square-sectioned oak pipe drilled out to a diameter of 11 cm (4½ in.) was found in an early fourteenth century but residual context.

Monasteries and water management

Hydraulic engineering for drainage and industry, though it did not demand clean water, was if anything more extensive, requiring vast earth-moving that has left its trace on the landscape. The Cistercians particularly are associated with dramatic exploitation of natural water courses for they more than any other order invested in monumental schemes of water management. This is seen at its best in the earthworks of Bordesley Abbey, in which the sequence of water management can be identified. A similar development can be read from the massive surviving earthworks at Rievaulx with the added bonus that they can be related to a surviving series of documents and closely dated (**62**). In 1131, the founder, Walter Espec, granted the Cistercians a site on the east bank of the River Rye, the land on the other bank belonging to Roger de Mowbray who subsequently gave it to the monks of Byland. As a result, the Rievaulx monks did not have full control of their river and could not exploit it to their advantage, though they did take a

sewer off it to flush their latrines. Before 1150, an agreement was reached with Byland allowing Rievaulx to divert the river to the west side of its valley, leaving its old course to be used as a controllable mill-leat. On this, three mills were built: a corn mill, a fulling mill and a water-powered smithy. This diversion was only the first stage in a well-planned operation, for by 1160 a second diversion was made possible by the grant of a further block of land by Hugh de Malbis.

Both this and the first grant from Byland had an added benefit of adding some 32 ha (80 acres) of water-meadow to the abbey precinct. This was not to be the end of the matter, for the house still did not have control of the river where it left the precinct, and Hugh's son Richard was persuaded to give the monks a block of land called 'Oswaldyngs' permitting a final realignment of the river to ensure total control of the Rye in the vicinity of the abbey. Over the same period, the monks of Byland were equally active, draining a new site for their house to provide massive ponds which collected water to power their mills and flush their latrines on a site which did not have the benefit of a powerful river. Their water engineering can still be traced from the monumental earthmoving it necessitated, and from post-suppression field names.

The most important use of flowing water, either in a river or diverted channel, was to flush the monks' communal latrine drains, and local conditions might involve the replanning

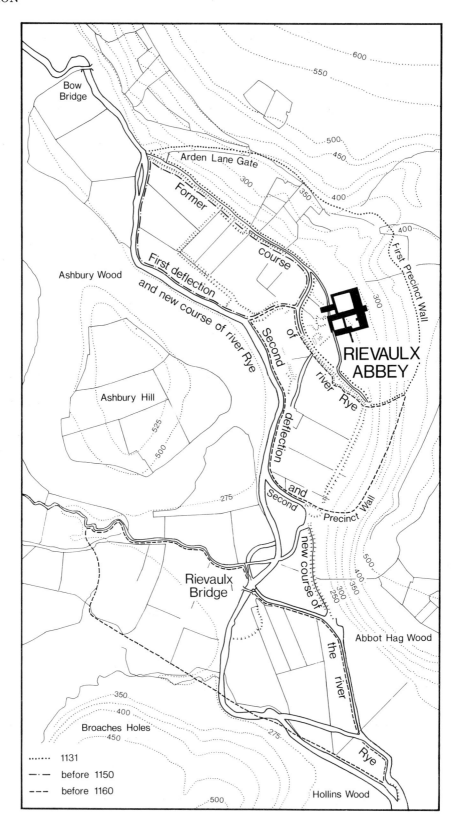

Bow
Bridge

Arden Lane Gate

Former

course

First deflection

Ashbury Wood

and new course of river Rye

Second

of

First Precinct Wall

river Rye

RIEVAULX
ABBEY

Ashbury Hill

deflection

and

Second

new course of

Precinct Wall

275

Rievaulx
Bridge

Abbot Hag Wood

the   river

Broaches Holes

Rye

.... 1131

—·—· before 1150

— — — before 1160

Hollins Wood

62 *The developing system of water management at Rievaulx Abbey can be identified from surviving earthworks and contemporary land grants.*

of the cloister ranges to take advantage of a natural water-course. At Easby Abbey this meant the placing of the canons' dormitory in the west range of the cloister so that the adjacent latrine block could efficiently use the fast-flowing waters of the River Swale. Normally, the latrines were flushed by a canalized drain in preference to the river itself as this permitted easier control of valuable water which might also be needed for mills and industrial use. Many of these great drains survive, often tall enough to walk in, with slabbed tops or tunnel vaults, and lined with well-dressed stone, reused for mansions that were built on the site of former monasteries in the sixteenth century. Knowledge of these has led to innumerable stories about tunnels leading from monastic sites. The tunnel that serviced the latrines at Easby survives, some 1.5 m (5 ft) high and with a bottom of flagstones. Few have been properly examined archaeologically, although the main drain of Norton Priory is a valuable exception. There, the sewer was traced for some 120 m (400 ft), and was found to flow

from east to west. In its original late-twelfth-century form, to the east of the latrine block the relatively small drain was stone-lined and square in section. Within the first phase of the latrine, however, it fed a timber drain, not lined with boards as might be expected but hollowed from tree-trunks 71 cm (28 in.) wide. The timber had been partially preserved by the waterlogging of the subsoil and by the realignment of the latrine block when it was rebuilt with a stone-lined drain in the late thirteenth or fourteenth century. This rebuilding necessitated the redirection of the drain to the west, and the new drain had a base consisting of sandstone blocks hollowed out to a semi-circular cross-section. At the east end of the latrine, a sluice was provided to control the head of water available for flushing the channel.

Latrines and sanitation

The twelfth-century latrine block at Rievaulx Abbey survives in part intact to its wall-plate,

63 *Cross section of (a) the monks' latrine block at Rievaulx Abbey and (b) the laybrothers' latrine block at Fountains Abbey show how the building functioned and give a clear impression of the scale of such essential buildings.*

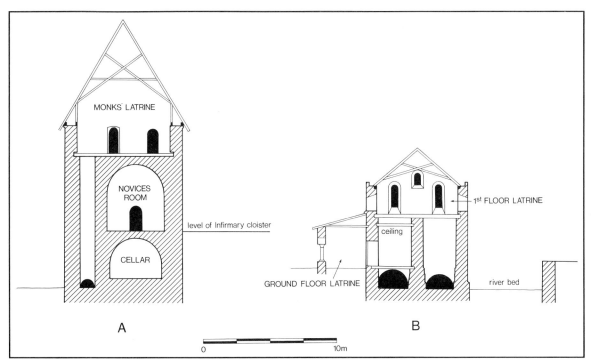

demonstrating the great scale of sanitary provision (**63a**) and comparable with the monks' latrine or *necessarium* of the Canterbury drawing. Built to serve a community of 140 monks in the early 1160s, it stands three storeys high on a terrace below the main monastic buildings. On its south side a narrow drain fed by a stone-lined channel that brought water from the old course of the River Rye was walled off from the two lower storeys, which comprised well-appointed and barrel-vaulted rooms used for the convent's domestic needs. Only the upper floor comprised the latrine, with wooden seats placed over the drain. Sockets in the masonry suggest partitioning for individual closets, although the total number can no longer be estimated. At Christchurch, Canterbury, there is evidence of 55 individual cubicles, at Lewes 30 and at Worcester 23. Two doors gave access to and from the dormitory, one to come and one to go. It is common to find an opening between the doors which contained a lamp to light the latrine and its access from the dormitory, as at Kirkham or Fountains, but it was not provided in this case. The drain continued as an open channel beyond the latrine block running back to the canalized original course of the River Rye (see **62**).

Though water was used to flush out the latrine drains, excavation has demonstrated on a number of occasions that it was not wholly effective, and the channel below the latrines also needed to be cleared by hand from time to time. All that survives of course is the debris that was building up at the time of the suppression for earlier deposits had already been removed. At Humberstone Abbey, where the water level was controlled by a wooden sluice, excavation recovered a substantial group of pottery from the latrine drain, all of it dating from the early sixteenth century. Most of the vessels were urinals that had been dropped accidentally into the drain from the latrine above. These are common finds on high-quality sites, and particularly so in a monastic context and their use is not only one of convenience. Urine was collected for tanning, and was used particularly in the production of vellum, the staple material used for monastic books. Clearly, urinals were placed in the latrines to collect urine rather than waste such a valuable commodity. The fecal waste from the latrine drain itself also had a use as fertilizer, and it is quite possible that it was purposely allowed

to build up within the drain, to be recovered and carted away as manure. The alternative to canalized sewers was the placing of the latrine block over an open watercourse, the option chosen at Fountains Abbey from the 1150s. Originally, a similar arrangement to that used at Rievaulx had been tried and apparently found wanting, and as the cloister buildings were being remodelled after a fire in 1146 the latrines were moved onto the River Skell that had been diverted round the early monastic buildings. The laybrothers' latrines survive virtually intact, showing precisely how they functioned (**63b**). Here, there were two separate drains, divided to first-floor level by a solid spine wall. In the south wall were a series of nine tall round-headed arches serving a series of latrines at ground-floor level. Originally these served the Outer Court which lay on the south bank of the river, but they were later enclosed within a pentice to serve the adjacent laybrothers' infirmary. Great timber joists, evidenced by their surviving sockets, spanned the channel and carried a series of wooden seats. At the east end of the block, further joist-holes indicate a ceiling or loft which only occupied the eastern end of the building. The northern channel served the upper floor which had a single door from the laybrothers' dormitory. The joist-sockets for this floor which spanned the whole building survive, though no trace remains of the seats which must have been ranged along the north wall. When this building was first erected there were at least 300 laybrothers at Fountains, of which 200 could have been accommodated in their great dormitory showing that the provision for the *conversi* was not as generous as that made for the choir-monks at Rievaulx.

Flushed sewers were the norm in monastic houses, but they did require expensive engineering which was not always affordable to smaller houses. One such case was found by excavation at St Leonard's Priory in Stamford where a large stone-lined pit was provided below the canons' latrines (**64**). Although provision was made for draining off fluids, the solid fecal matter remained within the pit and was dug out periodically, very much in the manner of urban cess-pits. In this case, the site lay next to the River Welland, and water-flushing would not have been a serious problem.

As well as the communal latrines provided for the cloister buildings, it is common to find individual latrines placed in all parts of the monastery. At Kirkham Priory for instance, excavation has revealed a latrine-shaft in a fourteenth-century sacristy attached to the north transept of the church, served by a cess-pit rather than a drain. At Fountains, Outer Court buildings such as the wool-house and malt-house, were provided with obedientiaries' offices with individual privies served by flushed drains, although pit-latrines are more common. At Thornholme Priory, pit-latrines were found serving the guesthouse and almonry, as well as a monumental latrine tower set over a pit serving chambers over the fourteenth-century gatehouse. The great late-fourteenth-century gatehouse at Thornton, with accommodation on three floors, was provided with no less than eight pit-privies, plus a further latrine in its secondary barbican, a fitting testimony to the sanitary provision that can be expected on a monastic site. Clean water and good drains were central to the monastic ideal.

64 *The pit below the latrine block at St Leonard's Priory at Stamford, with the blocking of a door in its south wall through which the pit could be periodically emptied (Christine Mahany).*

5

The precinct

Medieval monasteries were essentially self-contained and self-sustained institutions, depending for their continued existence on the produce and income of agricultural and industrial estates. Although the church and cloister were the heart of the monastery they comprised only a small part of the whole. Many other buildings were needed, either within the house or on its estates, to service the convent and to manage its economy. In effect, a monastery was a series of inwardly turned enclosures designed to protect the community from contact with the outside world. If the innermost enclosure was the cloister, the next was the Inner Court with its guest accommodation, granaries, bakehouse and brewhouse, often with its own gatehouse. Beyond this and contained within the precinct wall which enclosed the whole monastery was the Outer Court, which housed the agricultural and industrial buildings essential to the economic exploitation of the convent's estates. This was protected from the outside world by a gate. In general terms, the Outer Court was accessible to most people, whilst entry to the Inner Court was controlled more strictly. Beyond the monastery itself, the estates were managed either as granges, centralized and often specialist farms run directly by the convent, or as manors which were little different to those owned by laymen.

Although the Inner and Outer Courts made up at least three-quarters of the total area of the precinct, past concentration on the archaeology and architecture of the cloister buildings has left us largely ignorant of their nature. Few of their buildings survive, and fewer still have been excavated, although there have been notable exceptions. The clearest evidence of the nature of the monastic precinct can be found in the often detailed surveys of monastic houses made at the time of their suppression in the late 1530s.

The layout of the precinct

The whole precinct layout of the great Cistercian abbey of Rievaulx can be recovered from the evidence of four separate documents dating 1538–9. These comprise the initial grant of the suppressed abbey to its new owner, the Earl of Rutland, an inventory made before demolition began, a survey of the site during its spoliation, and the account rendered to the government at the end of Rutland's first year of ownership. In all, these documents describe the church, the cloister buildings, 27 other buildings in the Inner and Outer Courts, extensive watermeadows and other pasture fields (65). In particular we can identify three mills; the walk or fulling mill; the Iron Smiths', a smithy with water-powered hammers; and a corn mill. Additionally there are the extensive offices of the tannery or bark house, the houses of resident specialists such as the plumber, tanner, and smith, and close to the west range the brewhouse, bakehouse, kiln house and three other unidentified buildings. In the Outer Court there is the swine-house, the common stable, and the well-house, whilst other buildings listed include the Austell hall or guest-house, two gatehouses, and six tenanted properties, some of which housed pensioners or corrodians of the abbey. Also there was the gate chapel, which still survives, and at least 20 ha (50 acres) of water-meadows and pasture, some of which can still be identified on the ground and all within a stone precinct wall that can still be traced.

65 *The precinct of Rievaulx Abbey in 1538–9, defined by contemporary documents, surviving buildings and earthworks.*

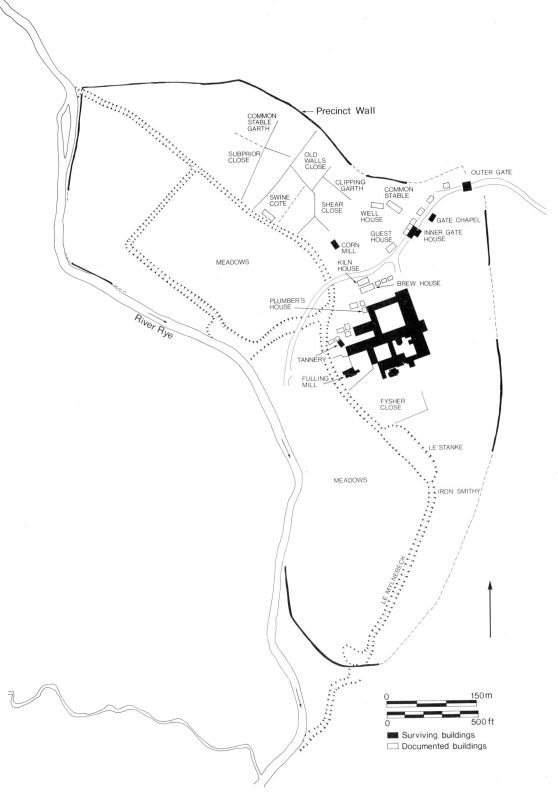

Precinct Wall

COMMON STABLE GARTH

SUBPRIOR CLOSE

OLD WALLS CLOSE

CLIPPING GARTH

COMMON STABLE

OUTER GATE

SWINE COTE

SHEAR CLOSE

WELL HOUSE

GATE CHAPEL

GUEST HOUSE

INNER GATE HOUSE

CORN MILL

MEADOWS

KILN HOUSE

BREW HOUSE

PLUMBER'S HOUSE

River Rye

TANNERY

FULLING MILL

FYSHER CLOSE

LE STANKE

IRON SMITHY

MEADOWS

LE MYLNEBECK

0   150 m

0   500 ft

■ Surviving buildings
□ Documented buildings

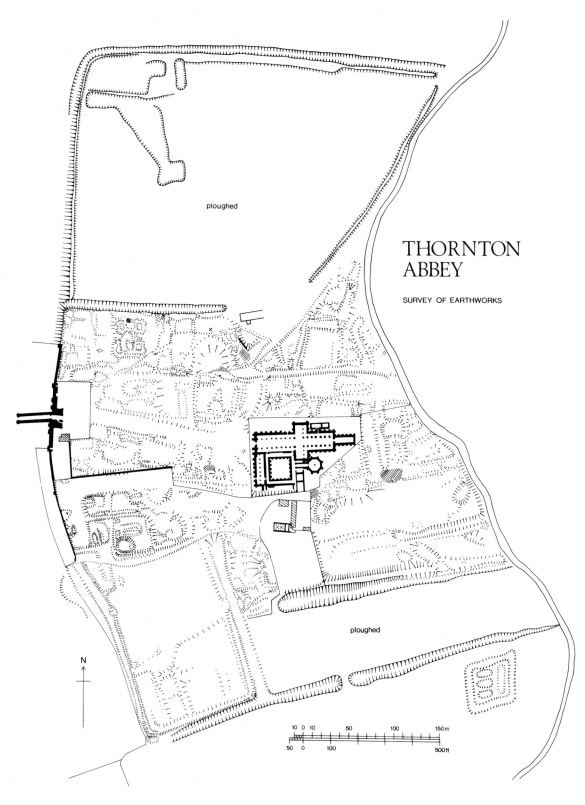

ploughed

THORNTON
ABBEY

SURVEY OF EARTHWORKS

ploughed

N

10 0 10   50   100   150m

50 0   100   500ft

66 *Surviving earthworks and surviving structures define the precinct and home grange of Thornton Abbey, one of the best-preserved monastic complexes in England (C. Atkins and D. Coppack).*

It must be remembered that Rievaulx was a large Cistercian house, with many specialist granges, and that most of its agricultural buildings, the barns and animal houses in particular, were not within the precinct but in the home granges that ringed the site. Most monasteries had a mixture of agricultural and industrial buildings within the precinct wall, but, as at Rievaulx, it is common to find meadowland, gardens and orchards as well.

Many precincts do survive complete as earthworks, however, and these can tell us a great deal about the layout and scale of the service areas in relation to the claustral nucleus. One of the finest surviving precincts is that of Thornton Abbey (**66**), a wealthy Augustinian house. Here the cloister buildings have been excavated and lie at the centre of an extensive precinct of 29 ha (71.7 acres) surrounded on three sides by a brick wall with square towers, strong gates and a water-filled ditch. On the north side is the home grange, the North Bail, which is an extension of the Outer Court. Field-walking on the south side of the site has also revealed extensive traces of medieval occupation apparently associated with the precinct and a fine group of fish ponds.

Within the precinct wall, the site is divided into a series of walled yards, many of which contain buildings of various sizes, though without excavation it is not possible to identify their use with any certainty. The Outer Court appears to be on the north side of the precinct, separated from the Inner Court by a surviving wall. Although documentary sources identify the existence of barns, granaries, the brew-house and bakehouse, and an extensive guest-house, and hint at a mill, their locations within the precinct remain largely unknown. Many more buildings can also be expected but cannot be traced from earthworks alone.

The Inner Court
No Inner Court has been fully examined archaeologically, although a number of examples survive, for instance at Lindisfarne Priory where it is enclosed within a strong wall that had its own gate, or at Mount Grace Priory where it comprises the southern part of the monastic enclosure. Individual buildings survive elsewhere or are known from documents.

The Commissioners for the *Valor Ecclesiasticus* travelling through Yorkshire in 1535 recorded in detail the monastic buildings they found, not only the major ranges but also the offices of the *curia*. One such surviving survey records the layout of the Benedictine nunnery of Wilberfoss in the Vale of York (see **20**). Here, nothing remains apart from the west part of the church, which was parochial, but the surveyors' description shows in graphic detail what can be expected of Inner Court buildings:

> Item the new garner [1] by the greate kychyn at th' este parte of the inner courte, xliiij foote longe and xv foote brode, tymbre walles, whitlymyd, and coueryd w^t slates.
> Item a workehouse [2] and a store house [3] vndir the same, besyde ij larder houses, tymber walles.
> Item the bakehouse [4] at the north parte of the courte, xx ffoote longe and xvj foote brode, tymber houses coueryd w^t slates.
> Item a little bultynge house [5] by the same.
> Item a pultrye house [6] xvj foote long and x foote brode.
> Item a garner ouer the same [7], xviij foote longe and xvj foote brode, coueryd w^t slates.
> Item a new parler [8] at the west parte of the courte, xxiiij foote longe and xvj foote brode, a chymney, tymber walles, a baye wyndo glasid conteyning (*blank*) foote of glasse, and seylid aboue.
> Item ij chambres [9 and 10] ouer the same w^t one chymney, one glasse wyndo of x foote of glass, and coueryd w^t tyles.
> Item the pristes chambre [11] w^{t}oute the gates, xx foote longe and xij foote brode, daubid walles, coueryd w^t thak.

Wilberfoss was a poor house in a part of the country without good building stone. Apart from its Inner Court buildings, all the claustral ranges with the exception of the church were also of timber, many of them described in the survey as new and clearly of good status. Thus the use of timber for the Inner Court does not imply buildings of a second quality. The new parlour with its two upper chambers can be identified as the guest-house with little difficulty, close to the court gate, and next to a first floor granary with two rooms below, for poultry and for the storage and sifting of flour.

The bakehouse completed the range and almost certainly was combined with a brewhouse on the Lindisfarne model. The new granary on the east side of the court, set over a workhouse, store-room and two larders formed the link with the cloister, being connected with the convent kitchen. The provision of a priest's house at the entrance to the Inner Court is normal in the layout of a nunnery, for the priest was the one member of the community who had regular contact with the outside world. Placing his house directly outside the court gate effectively gave him control over who had access to the cloister.

A small number of Inner Court buildings are known from excavation, the most frequently studied being guest-houses, buildings which were often architecturally sophisticated and which tend to survive. Excavation of the guest-house complex at Kirkstall Abbey from 1979 to 1987 revealed an extensive group of buildings centred on a great aisled hall of the early thirteenth century. Largely reduced to low walling, it was possible for the excavators to identify three principal phases of development in what was a much rebuilt structure (**67**). As originally built, the guest-house comprised a substantial timber-framed aisled hall of four bays set on cill walls, with an open central hearth and a service wing at its south end. A wall fireplace at the north end of the hall suggests that the northern bay was partitioned

off as a sleeping chamber. To the south of the hall block was a detached kitchen, and against its south-east corner were the fragmentary remains of a bakehouse, perhaps part of the bakehouse and brewhouse normally found in the Inner Court. The establishment was provided with a piped water supply. In plan, the guest-house resembled a large manor house, reflecting the quality of society it was provided to serve.

In the late thirteenth century, the accommodation was substantially improved. The main hall was rebuilt in stone with the addition of a two-storey chamber block at its north end. At the south end, the service block was rebuilt as a cross-wing with additional chambers at first-floor level and one on the ground floor. The main monastic drain was diverted to run down the west side of the guest-house to serve latrine towers attached to both chamber blocks. To the south, the bakehouse was extended and a scullery provided. More significantly, a subsidiary hall was provided to the west to cater for less socially advantaged visitors. Like the first phase of the main hall, it was a timber-framed structure with an open central hearth. In the fourteenth century its north end was

67 *The ground plan of the Kirkstall guest-house (a) in the early thirteenth century, (b) in the late thirteenth century, and (c) in the fifteenth century.*

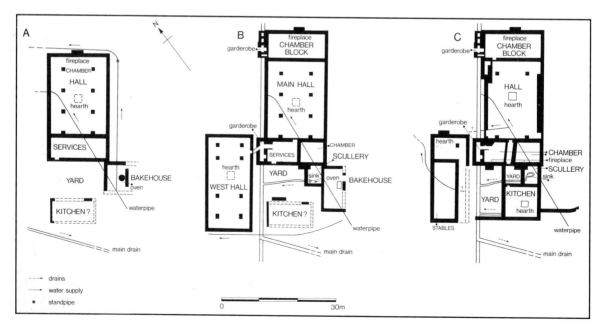

provided with its own hearth and was partitioned off to provide a separate chamber.

The final phase of reorganization dated to the fifteenth century, and demonstrated that the guest-house had been constantly improved throughout its life. The main hall was substantially rebuilt in stone, with most of its aisle posts removed, indicating a new roof. An internal stair was provided to the upper floor of the northern chamber block and a wall-bench built against the east wall. The old service wing was further adapted to provide additional chamber space, and a new square-plan kitchen was built to the south, separated from the main building by a small yard. The secondary or west hall was changed out of all recognition: its west aisle was demolished, and the greater part of its nave converted to use as a stable. The northern two bays were then fitted up as a smithy.

Social distinction in the guest accommod-ation of greater monasteries is common, the quality of buildings being graded according to status. At Fountains Abbey, two guest-houses of the mid-twelfth century show this clearly (**68**). Both provided a different form of accommodation to the common guest-hall and private chambers found at Kirkstall. Instead, each of the two guest-houses has separate facilities on both the ground and the first floor comprising a hall, a chamber and a latrine, the lower storey being vaulted. The east guest-house provided the better quality accommodation, with both hall and chamber occupying three bays of the

68 *At Fountains Abbey two guest-houses of the mid twelfth century are amongst the finest surviving domestic buildings of any monastery. Unlike the common guest-hall at Kirkstall they provide four separate suites for visitors of the highest rank.*

building. The vault of the lower floor was supported on finely moulded ribs, and a wall-fireplace, its now missing hood supported on detached shafts with waterleaf capitals, was provided in the upper bay of the hall. The upper floor, of which only the gable walls survive, mirrored the ground-floor arrangement but, being open to the roof and additionally lit by rose windows in its gables, was of better quality. The west guest-house was still substantial though smaller, being only four bays long and divided equally into hall and chamber, and the architectural detailing was more restrained. Again, the upper floor was of better quality, showing that four grades of high status guest-house were available from about 1160.

69 *The late twelfth-century guest-house at Thornholme Priory, a plan recovered by excavation.*

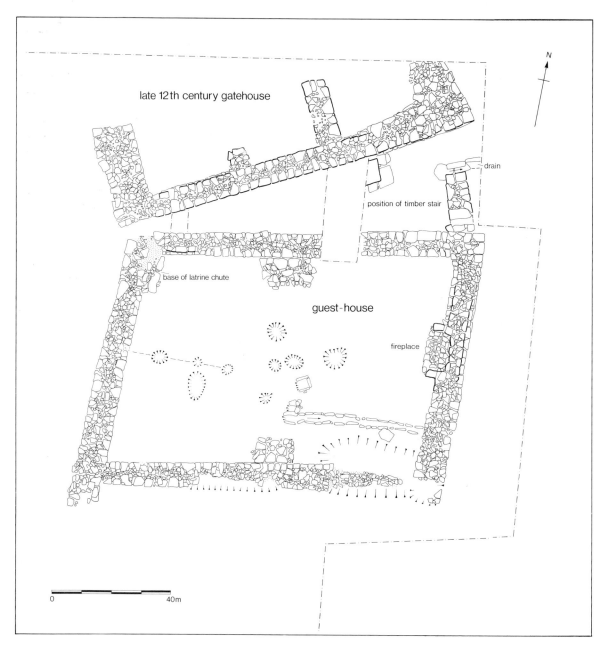

As at Kirkstall, the Fountains guest-houses were extended and modernized throughout the medieval period, though their twelfth-century shells were retained. The 'Austell Hall' of the Rievaulx survey must disguise a substantial establishment following one of these models. Additionally, poorer quality lodging was provided for the lower levels of travelling society. At Fountains, documents tell us of a common dormitory, the 'poor mans house', attached to the almonry at the entrance to the Inner Court.

Hospitality was central to monastic life, and guest-houses were amongst the first buildings to be provided in a new monastery. St Aelred, visiting the new Cistercian mission centre of Rievaulx within two years of its foundation, was lodged in a timber guest-house which he saved from fire. Excavation at Thornholme Priory revealed a guest-house built in about 1170 (**69**) at the entrance to the precinct. Stratigraphically, it could be shown to be earlier than the priory gatehouse which was built alongside it, a sure indication of the relative importance of the two buildings, and its architectural detail shows it to be contemporary with the priory church.

Thornholme was a middle-rank house of average means, so its buildings are more likely to be typical than those of wealthy houses like Kirkstall or Fountains. Following the near-contemporary Fountains model, the Thornholme guest-house was a masonry building with separate accommodation on two floors,

though it had been reduced to its lowest courses by stone robbing. The building was of fine quality but of a different tradition to those at Kirkstall and Fountains, using coursed limestone rubble and ashlar dressings, all of which had been removed by stone robbers. Excavation recovered quantities of lime plaster indicating that the rubble walls were plastered inside and out and painted with limewash in much the same way as the Fountains buildings. Some fragments had traces of lining in red paint, suggesting that the outside at least was painted to resemble good quality freestone. Smaller than the Fountains guest-houses, it was still a substantial building some 12.8 m (42 ft) long and 8.3 m ($27\frac{1}{2}$ ft) wide internally. Stone thresholds indicated centrally placed doors in the north and south walls at ground level, and the base of a timber stair outside the north-east corner of the building located the entrance to the upper floor there. In the north-west corner of the structure an internal widening of the foundations marked the position of a latrine chute serving the upper floor, which may have provided better quality accommodation. The

70 *A reconstruction of the guest-house range and attached bakehouse and brewhouse at Mount Grace Priory, based on the remains of those buildings contained within a post-suppression mansion.*

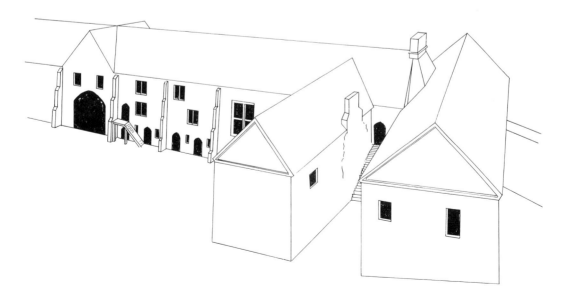

ground floor was partitioned into four separate rooms by timber screening, located by the settings of its earthfast posts, and a stone-lined drain was provided, running from the centre of the building to discharge outside the east wall. The domestic nature of the ground floor was demonstrated by the insertion of a fine fireplace in the east gable wall at the very end of the twelfth century.

Guest accommodation varied considerably as the early fifteenth century guest-wing at Mount Grace Priory shows. Enclosing the Inner Court to the north of its gatehouse, the guest-house range has survived largely intact within a post-suppression house of 1654 (**70** and **72**). In spite of its dramatic remodelling it remains principally a building of the 1420s. The east wall survives virtually intact with numerous primary window and door openings, and critical areas of the west wall, which retains its original buttresses, also survive the seventeenth-century refenestration. No trace whatsoever remains of any original masonry cross walls within the building, and it seems likely that the internal partitions were of timber. As originally built, it comprised accommodation for guests in the form of four individual suites at ground storey, each with a plain chamfered four-centred door and a single square-headed light facing onto the Inner Court, with accommodation of a better quality on the floors above. The chambers associated with the upper suite appear to have comprised a third floor which occurred only at the south end of the building. The windows of the upper suite were all of two lights below a square head. Access to the upper suite was by means of a wooden stair from the Inner Court.

To the north of the guest suites was a hall open to the roof, with tall transomed windows in both east and west walls which cut across the floor levels of the remainder of the building. This hall, which presumably served the guests, was entered by a door in its south-west corner which gave onto a screens passage with a loft above it. To the north of the hall, the range was of two storeys, with a kitchen on the ground floor and two chambers above. This part of the range retains all of its medieval features, lying outside the post-medieval house until 1900–1. The kitchen, like the hall, was entered from the Inner Court, and its floor level was approximately 45 cm (18 in.) above that of the hall, following a rise in ground level. Above

the kitchen were two chambers. That to the south was entered by an external stair rising from the Outer Court to the west. The northern room, apparently a bed chamber, had a stair rising from the Inner Court to the east alongside a now-demolished wing.

At the north end of the range was a substantial cross-wing which comprised the second group of Inner Court buildings. The western part was the brewhouse with a great embattled chimney still standing to full height in its south-west corner, which it shared with the guest-house kitchen to the south. The eastern part, demolished to ground level, was the bakehouse. As originally built, the cross-wing was of two storeys, and the north face of the chimney has a number of blocked sockets that show the form of the roof. The building was excavated in 1900 and its internal layout largely recovered. A polygonal kiln with substantial buttresses was inserted into the east wall of the brewhouse and, judging from its scale, was probably a two-storey structure. The bakehouse was separated from the brewhouse by a solid masonry wall and was floored with stone flags. Traces of a partition remained, dividing the room into two. Like the brewhouse it was entered by a door in its north wall, close to which was an inserted bread-oven. Opposite these was a large inserted fireplace. Clearly the room had been adapted from some previous use.

The bakehouse at Thornholme Priory was a thirteenth-century conversion of an earlier building (**71**). It remains one of only three monastic bakehouses to have been excavated in recent years, the others being at Bradwell Abbey and Grove Priory. The principal feature of the building was a large sub-circular bread-oven against the east wall which made use of an earlier chimney flue. This was rebuilt or repaired on at least two occasions. Its fill comprised many fine layers of wood-ash, the residue of numerous firings. The rest of the building was provided with heavy-duty pitched limestone floors which included a drain, and two small rooms were partitioned at the west end. One was presumably where the bolting hutch was kept for the sifting of meal during the making of bread. An internal stair on the north side of the building gave separate access to the upper floor, the use of which is unknown.

For the remaining buildings of the Inner Court, the best evidence is provided by the surviving ranges at Mount Grace Priory (**72**).

71 *The thirteenth-century bakehouse at Thornholme Priory contained a single large sub-circular bread oven against its east wall filled with many layers of wood ash left by continuous firings, and had heavy stone floors.*

Ranged around three sides of a yard are the remains of five separate two-storey buildings in addition to the guest-house range and gatehouse. All were built in the fifteenth or early sixteenth centuries and show a progression from timber to stone construction. The upper floors were all granaries, indicating the scale of grain production and consumption in a wealthy monastery. At ground floor, however, was a series of separate offices. In the west range were four small rooms divided by timber partitions. In the south range, the first ground-floor room on the west is featureless, and was most probably a store. The next room to the east was a stable with floor-drains. Slots in its south wall indicate the positions of three mangers. To the east was a ground-floor granary that served the kiln-house, normally associated with malting barley for brewing. The ghost of the kiln itself remains in the floor. The building on the east

side of the court remains to be excavated, and its ground-floor arrangements are unknown.

The Outer Court

The Outer Court which provided the economic base of the monastery was largely ignored until the 1970s, though this situation has been partly rectified by a series of excavations at Waltham Abbey, Thornholme Priory, Fountains Abbey and Grove Priory. Its buildings were largely agricultural or industrial, as can be seen from the suppression survey of Wilberfoss Priory:

> Item ane oxe-house and ij stables vndir ane hole roof, lxx foote longe and xvj foote brode, daubid walles, coueryd with thak.
> Item ane old swynecote, xij foote longe and viij foote brode, brokyn walles, coueryd w^t thak, decayed.
> Item a corne barne, xx/iiij xvj foote longe and xviij foote brode, dawbid walles, coueryd w^t thak.
> Item ane old barne to ley turfes yn, xxiiij foote longe and xx foote brode, brokyn walles, coueryd w^t thak, decayed.
> Item a dovecote, x ffoote square, mudde walles, coueryd w^t thak.

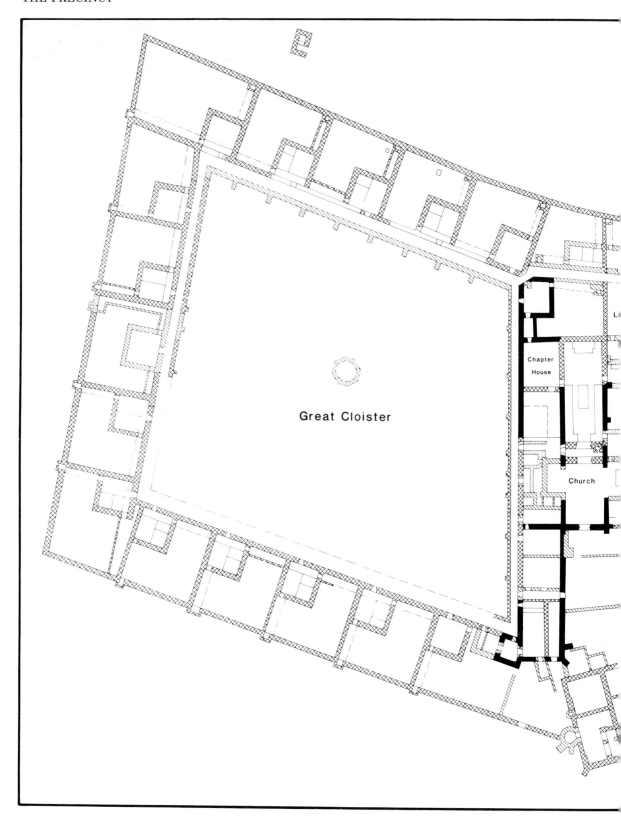

Great Cloister

Chapter
House

Church

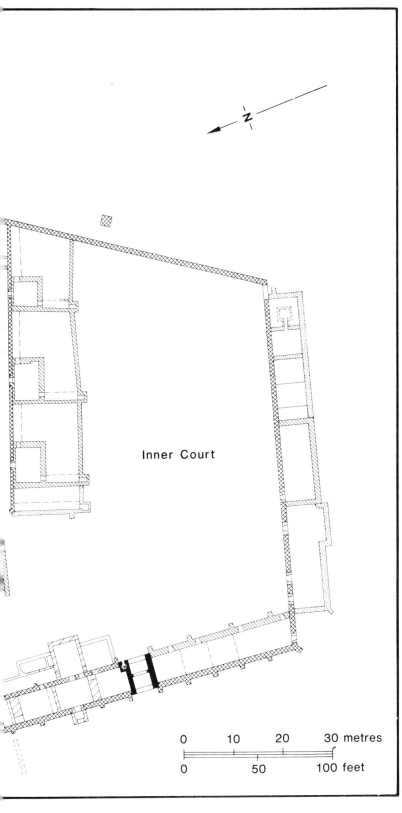

Inner Court

0   10   20   30 metres

0   50   100 feet

Item a kylne house, xvj foote longe and x foote brode, dawbid walles, coueryd w^t thak. Item ane orchard where the dovecote standith.

The Outer Court of a small nunnery such as Wilberfoss might be seen as providing the basic

73 *In the late twelfth century, the south-west corner of the precinct at Thornholme Priory contained a two-storey building (Ci) of high status, perhaps the house of the priory steward. In a small yard to its east was an earlier dovecot (Ei).*

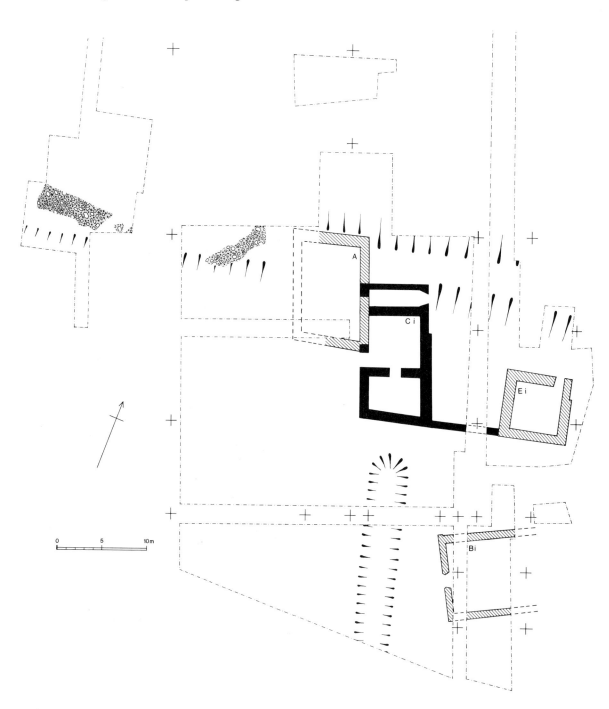

minimum of services. The Rievaulx surveys include details of mills, an extensive tannery, and the offices of the smith and convent plumber. Some buildings survive in recognizable form – the water mills of Fountains, Jervaulx, Monk Bretton and Abbotsbury; barns

74 *The steward's hall at Thornholme in the thirteenth century was a great timber-framed aisled building of at least four bays (Biii), rebuilt on three occasions before it was finally converted into a granary.*

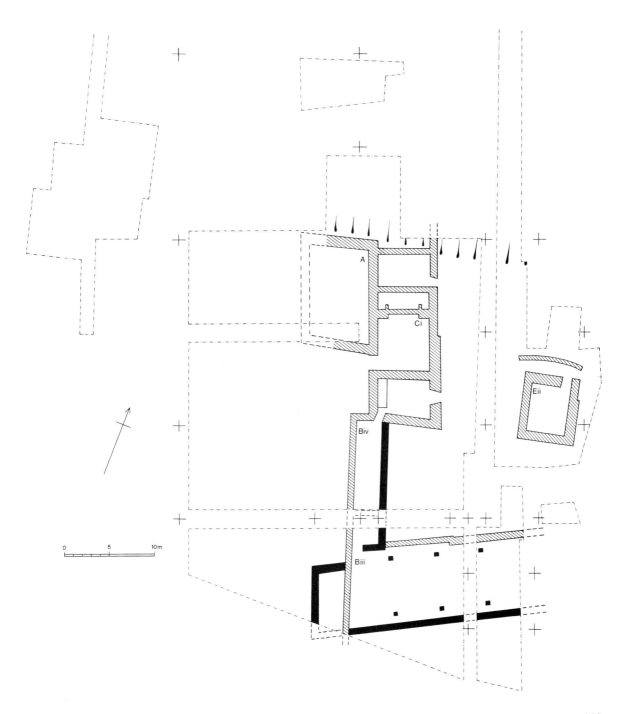

at Watton Priory, Temple Cressing, Titchfield Abbey and Bradenstoke Priory, and the dovecot at Garway. More are known from excavation, particularly at Thornholme and Grove Priories, and Fountains and Waltham Abbeys, including barns, granaries, dovecots and industrial buildings. At Fountains these include the great woolhouse that comprised an essential part of the monastery's early economy, whilst at Thornholme Priory excavation also recovered the full structural history of the gatehouse to the precinct and its attached almonry and gate chapel. Excavation has also revealed buildings that are neither agricultural nor industrial.

At Thornholme Priory, a series of high-quality domestic halls were found amongst agricultural buildings in the south-west corner of the precinct, ranging in date from the 1170s to the early fourteenth century. The earliest of these, Building C(i) (73), was a building of the highest quality judging from its remaining architectural detail, with a hall and chamber at first-floor level reached by an enclosed stair against its north gable wall. The two ground-floor rooms were simply store or service rooms

entered from a yard on the west side of the building, whilst entry to the domestic accommodation was from an enclosed yard to the east, which also contained a dovecot. This building was replaced by an important aisled hall of at least four bays in the early thirteenth century on a new site to the south (74), with an open hearth set in the floor at its west or upper end. This building was rebuilt on three occasions before being converted to a granary. From the high quality of the buildings, it has been suggested that they were the houses of the steward, a lay official responsible for the administration and exploitation of the priory estates. They do not stand alone, for a similar aisled building is known in the Outer Court at Elstow Abbey, and another domestic hall has been recorded in the Veresmead or Outer Court at Waltham Abbey, and was later converted to agricultural use.

75 *The first of two phases of dovecot excavated at Thornholme Priory and dating to the third quarter of the twelfth century.*

Dovecots providing a supply of fresh meat were common on monastic sites, though few have been excavated. The Thornholme dovecot, Building E(i) (**73** and **75**), was one of the first stone buildings to be erected in the Outer Court and was contemporary with the guest-house described above (p. 107). It was partially rebuilt in the early fourteenth century but had fallen out of use by the middle of the fifteenth century. The earliest building was 7.5 m (24 ft) square with plastered walls painted in imitation of ashlar and a tiled hipped roof with decorated ridge tiles. Within, tiers of nesting boxes occupied each wall from just above floor level. The floor itself was of mortar, scoured hollow with the constant collection of guano. A drain leading to a tank outside the east wall also served to collect this valuable commodity, which was especially valued for the preparation of parchment skins. Excavation recovered not only the plan of a remarkable building but also the remains of many of the birds that were kept there. Because the building had been kept clean, the occurrence of so many dead birds on its final floor surface suggested some type of avian epidemic. The building was abandoned, to be replaced by a circular dovecot still visible as an earthwork on another part of the site.

Excavation at Waltham Abbey also produced evidence of two dovecots in the Veresmead: a fragmentary circular structure of twelfth-century date, and a superimposed square building of the fifteenth century. The later building had a central socket for a potence, the revolving frame against which a ladder could be placed, a feature repeated in the fourteenth-century rebuilt dovecot at Thornholme. The circular dovecot built by the Knights Hospitlar at Garway in 1326 demonstrates the most common form with tiers of nesting-boxes divided into groups of four by plain string-courses. A central tank 1.5 m (5 ft) in diameter was provided in the floor to collect guano, and stone-built drains ran from this tank to a larger collecting pit.

The mill was central to the monastic economy, and, given the preference for siting monasteries on rivers, water-mills were often provided within the Outer Court. The finest surviving example is the great double corn mill at Fountains (**76**), on the face of it an early-thirteenth-century building which incorporates earlier masonry. It has recently been the subject of detailed archaeological study and, although it has yet to be excavated, for the first time it is

possible to disentangle its structure and identify no fewer than three distinct buildings.

The earliest building, represented by its east and south walls, each with a surviving window, dated from the late 1130s. The visible masonry belongs to the upper floor of the building and survives to wall-plate level. The lower storey, which had a wheel at its south end driven by a surviving race, was buried in the 1150s when a new mill was built. This mill was set on a dam to create a mill-pond that powered an undershot wheel in the old race to the south and a breast-shot wheel at the north end of the building. The ground floor of the first mill was buried within the dam, and the east wall of the upper floor was retained to support the east wall of the new mill, enclosing its basement and wheel-pits. The new building had round-headed doors and single-light windows, none of which survives. They were converted to two-light windows in the thirteenth century, one jamb coursed with the twelfth century wall and one very clearly inserted. The early-thirteenth-century rebuilding added an upper storey granary to the old mill and extended it at the north end, where it was of two rather than three storeys. Additionally, a building, now lost, was built against its south-east corner in the fourteenth century. Apart from the insertion of new window heads in the ground floor windows of the west elevation and some internal partitioning in the early eighteenth century, the mill remained unaltered and in use until 1937, almost eight centuries after the first part was built.

Unlike the Fountains water-mill, the abbey woolhouse is known only from excavation. Identified by Hope as the bakehouse in the 1880s, it was re-excavated in the late 1970s to reveal a great aisled storehouse reduced almost totally to low walling (**77**). It proved to be a complex structure, part of a massive range of buildings that included the malthouse and brewhouse, with six principal phases of construction from its first building in the 1150s to its eventual demolition in the late fifteenth century. Essentially it was a great barn with an office for the obedientiary attached to its north-east corner. As the abbey's economy developed throughout the thirteenth century it was enlarged and, by the end of the century, had acquired a fulling mill in its western aisle powered by an undershot wheel. The malthouse and brewhouse to the south were also rebuilt

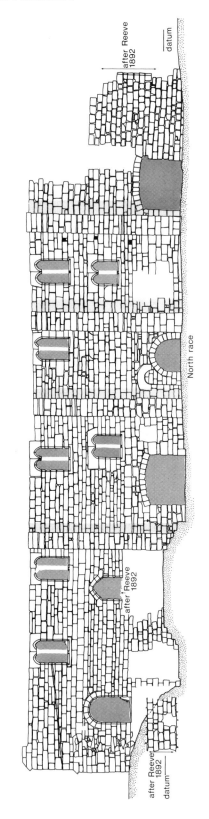

EAST ELEVATION: medieval masonry

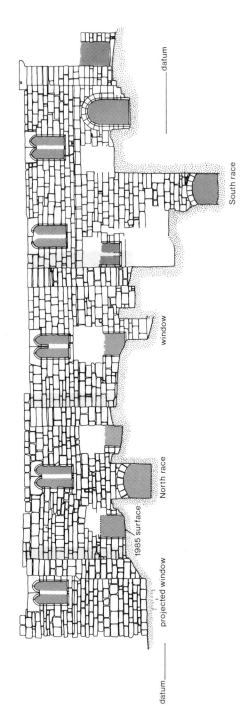

WEST ELEVATION: medieval masonry

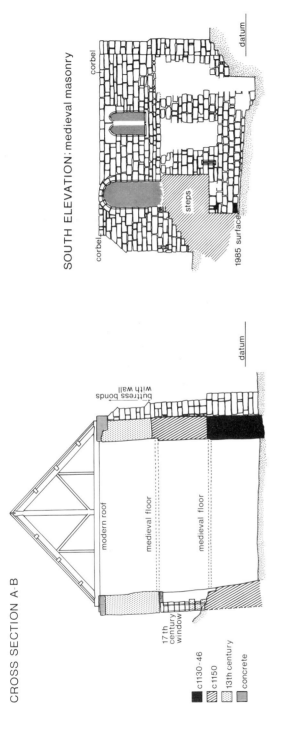

CROSS SECTION A-B

SOUTH ELEVATION: medieval masonry

corbel

corbel

corbel

steps

1985 surface

datum

buttress bonds
with wall

modern roof

medieval floor

medieval floor

17th
century
window

datum

c1130-46
c1150
13th century
concrete

metres

0 1 2 3 4 5 10

76 *A survey of the medieval masonry of the Fountains mill shows that it was originally built in the 1130s, rebuilt in the 1150s and substantially extended and remodelled in the 1220s. Traces of long-demolished fourteenth century buildings remain in its east wall.*

77 *The Fountains wool-house as excavated was a building of many phases reduced for the most part to low walling and foundations.*

at this period. The fourteenth century saw changes in the use of the building with the insertion of dye-vats in the remains of the fulling mill and the provision of two furnaces to provide hot water. The western aisles were partitioned off and appear to have been used for the finishing of cloth. This was no longer the woolhouse, but a multi-purpose structure.

Its final use came in the mid fifteenth century when it was partitioned up as workshops used for a restoration of the abbey church. Debris indicated glaziers at work in the central part of the building, whilst a small blacksmith's forge was created in the eastern aisle, the smith's tongs and the lead lining of his water boshes still lying in the hammer-scale on the floor. To the south of the smithy was a pit full of bronze-working debris. In the last quarter of the fifteenth century the building had outlived its usefulness and was demolished, leaving the malthouse standing alone. The site was simply levelled and only good walling-stone removed.

Almost all the architectural detail was thrown down close to its original location, permitting an accurate reconstruction of the building to be made (**78**).

Smithies were necessary to service not only the builders of monasteries but also the agricultural needs of the community, and were thus commonly provided. At Waltham Abbey, a substantial smithy has been excavated in the Outer Court (**79**). Although it had a complicated structural history it appears to have had at least two hearths, with hoods and bellows placings demonstrated by post-holes. Clay-lined pits in the floor served as water boshes for quenching the hot iron and in several instances had been filled with bloomery waste, showing that iron was also smelted nearby. One small hearth set in the floor had even been used to smelt lead on a small scale.

More common and a necessary part of an agricultural economy were the granaries best known from Thornholme Priory. Although they are often described as first-floor structures in suppression period surveys, this was not always the case. The fourteenth-century granary at Thornholme (**80**) was a ground-floor structure

78 *From fallen architectural elements and the plan recovered by excavation, it was possible to reconstruct the appearance of the Fountains wool-house, shown here as it was in the fourteenth century.*

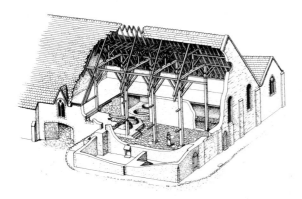

with a narrow corridor on its south side giving access to a series of bins divided by timber partitions, which were only apparent as slight depressions in the clay floor. Across the yard from the granary was the priory kiln-house (**81**), with its raised kiln surviving almost to full height. Grain was spread on the floor to dry in gentle heat before it was stored in the granary as damp grain could not be stored. A second grain drier belonging to the same phase of building was provided just outside the precinct wall to the west. A third was provided

79 *The smithy at Waltham Abbey as excavated is typical of the continuous modification or even rebuilding found in Outer Court buildings (after Huggins).*

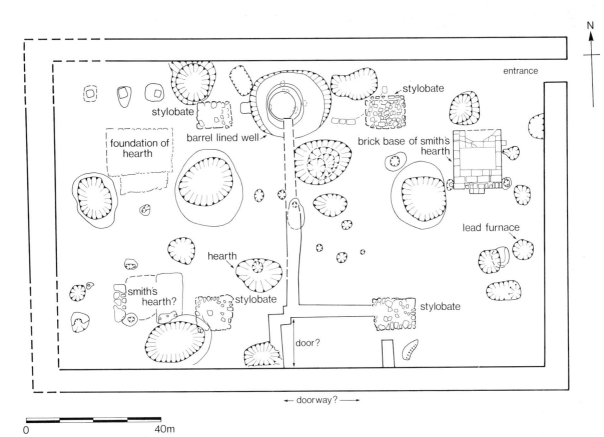

N

entrance

stylobate

stylobate

foundation of hearth

barrel lined well

brick base of smith's hearth

lead furnace

hearth

smith's hearth?

stylobate

stylobate

door?

← doorway? →

0   40m

80 *A late-fourteenth-century granary at Thornholme Priory in the south-west corner of the precinct, reusing the shell of an earlier aisled hall.*

elsewhere. The sudden appearance of granaries and grain driers in the second half of the fourteenth century suggests that there had been a major change in the priory's economy. Perhaps functions that had been carried out on outlying estates were then being tenanted rather than farmed in hand. Unless rent was being paid in grain, the outlying granaries and grain driers on tenanted lands may have been no longer accessible to the monastery.

The Outer Court was contained within the precinct wall, often a substantial boundary. Access to the precinct was controlled by one or more gatehouses. The main gatehouse at Thornholme has been excavated, revealing three phases of development (**82**) from the beginning of the thirteenth to the mid fourteenth centuries. The plans revealed are typical of

many surviving examples, but the value of the Thornholme excavation is that it has shown how complicated the sequence of events leading up to the construction of a surviving gate might be. Outside the gate was the gate-chapel for the use of visitors, including women who were excluded from the precinct, and the almonry, where food and alms were dispensed. This last building (**83**) had a central hall with wall benches and an open hearth, with service rooms south of a cross-passage, and a chamber at its north end. First built in the late fourteenth century, it was modified twice before 1536.

The home grange
The buildings of the precinct served the immediate needs of the community and they in turn were supported by a network of agricultural and industrial estates, held as either blocks of land or individual holdings spread across many manors and vills. Their extent and method of management resulted both from the wealth or otherwise of individual houses and the policy

81 *The kiln-house at Thornholme Priory, built in the late fourteenth century and being repaired at the suppression in 1536. The floor around the kiln would have been raised and has been removed by excavation to reveal the kiln structure.*

pursued by particular orders. Whilst the Benedictines and Augustinians were prepared to hold land in much the same way as lay magnates, the Cistercians rejected tenurial farming as late as the end of the thirteenth century in favour of a centralized economy staffed by laybrothers. Whatever the system chosen, estates were centred on farms or granges. In all but the poorest houses, the principal centre was the home grange, built close to the house and containing major barns and animal houses for which there was too little space within the precinct. Richard Pollard described the home grange of Bridlington Priory in 1537 thus:

82 *The three gatehouses built at Thornholme Priory between 1202 and the mid fourteenth century show a form of development that is typical of many monasteries.*

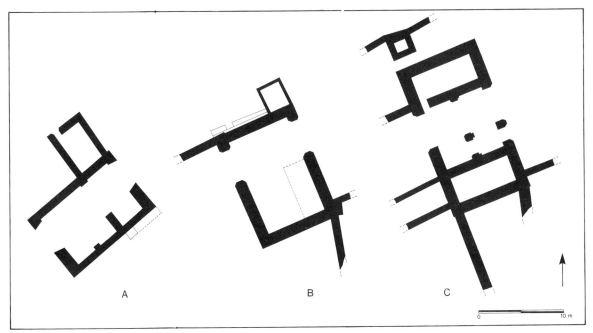

A   B   C

0   10 m

THE BARNE YARDE

It' there ys a great Barne Yarde on the Northsyde of the seyde Pryorye cont' by estymacyon foure Acres.

THE BARNE

It'm there ys on the Northsyde of the seyde Barne Yarde a very fayre Barne conteynyng in length Est & West, Cxvij pac's, and in breddith xxvij pac's well covered with lede to the value of fyve hundred m'ks, and so yt ys offered for.

THE GARNERD

It' on the South syde of the same Barne standyth a Garnerd to lay Corne in, conteynyng in length North and South, xxvj yards, and in breddith x yards covered with lede.

THE MALTHOUSE

It' on the Est syde of the same Garnerd standyth the Malthouse cont' in length North & South xliiij yerds, and in breddith xvij yards, well covered w^t lede; and on the North syde of the same Malthouse standyth a prety Howse with a Chamber where the Hervest men dyd alwayes dyne, covered with slatt.

THE KYLNE HOUSE

It'm on the Est syde of the same Malthouse standith a Kylne House covered with slatt.

OLDE STABLES & OXESTALLES

It'm on the Est & West syde of the Barne Yarde standyth olde Stables, Oxestalles, w^t other olde houses buylded w^t stone, covered with slatt, greatly in decaye.

Only one home grange has been examined in any detail. At Waltham Abbey rescue excavation in advance of road building in Grange Yard led to the recovery of ten buildings in far from ideal conditions (84). The scale and layout of the establishment was very similar to Pollard's record of Bridlington and included an aisled barn of 12 bays, some 64 m (210 ft) long, the hay barn, the plough-house, the ox-house, and a stable ranged about an open yard. The buildings ranged in date from the early thirteenth to the late fifteenth centuries and

83 *The almonry hall outside the gatehouse at Thornholme in the course of excavation. This building was altered or rebuilt at least twice in little more than a century.*

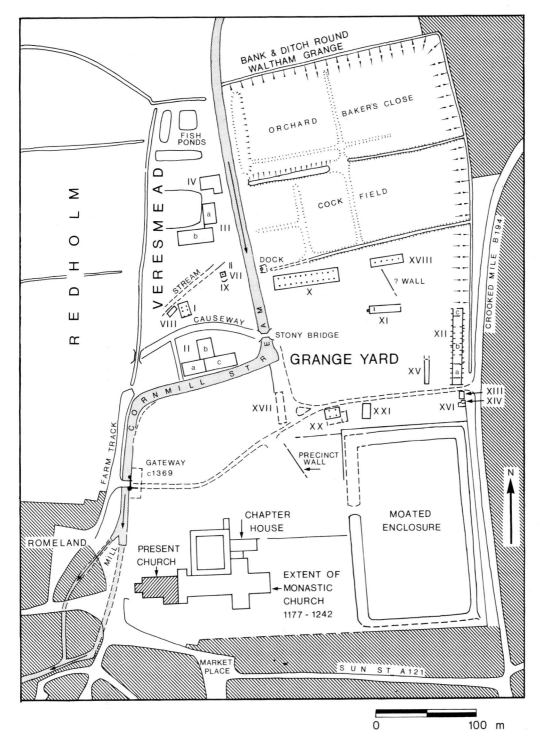

84 *The plan of Grange Yard at Waltham Abbey showing buildings known from excavation, parchmarks in the turf, and documents (after Huggins).*

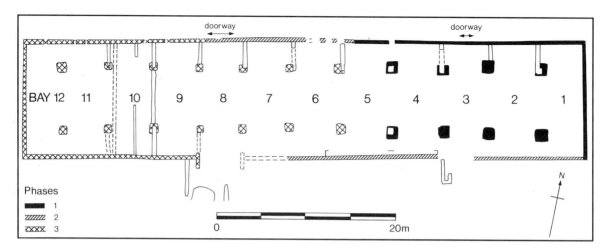

85 *The great barn in Grange Yard, Waltham (after Huggins).*

showed considerable evidence of reconstruction. Some had survived the suppression, being of use to the new lay owner of the site. The barn (**85**) was originally only of five bays and dated to the early years of the thirteenth century, extended by a further seven bays in the course of the thirteenth century as the abbey's economy was developed. Its storage capacity has been calculated at 8300 cubic m (90,000 cubic ft), and it would have been required to store the produce of a demesne estate of 418 ha (1033 acres) of arable land, up to one-third of which would have been fallow. The smaller haybarn, XVIII, in comparison was supported by 80 ha (198 acres) of meadow land. The plough-house, XI, like the barns was a timber-framed building on cill-walls, and dated from the fifteenth century. Its use – to store agricultural equipment – could be ascertained

only from a suppression period survey of the grange. The ox-house, XII, (**86**), also built in the fifteenth century, was perhaps the most remarkable of the grange buildings. At the south end was a hall with a large fireplace and a chamber, presumably the lodging of the bailiff. The building was aisled, as evidenced by the bases of arcade posts in the hall and by short walls that ran from the side walls of the ox-house itself to the line of the arcades. Remarkably, the position of the arcade posts did not tally with the external buttresses. The stalls for the oxen were ranged down both sides of the body of the building and were roughly a perch ($5\frac{1}{2}$ yd/5 m) wide, sufficient for four oxen, room for 32 beasts or eight teams in bays 6 to 9, or the 19 oxen and 13 work-horses recorded at the grange in 1540. At the north end of the building in bay 1 was a small grain-drier or malting kiln. In all, this was a multi-purpose

86 *The ox-house in Grange Yard, Waltham (after Huggins).*

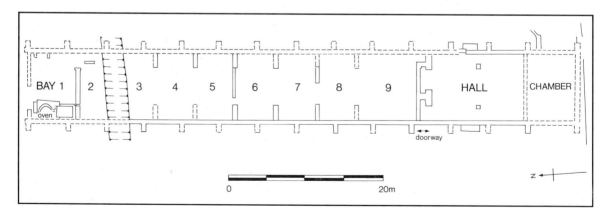

structure of a type common in suppression period surveys.

Distant granges

The greater houses might have more than one home grange, Fountains Abbey for instance had three – Morker, Fountains Park and Swanley – ringing the site on the south, west, and north sides. Most monasteries that derived their wealth from the land had several granges at a distance from the house, forming self-contained estate centres. It has long been assumed that these granges represented monasteries in miniature with a chapel and domestic ranges at the centre set around a cloister, and with agricultural buildings in an outer enclosure. Such an arrangement would particularly suit the Cistercians, who ran their estates with

87 *The central buildings of the Gorefields grange were laid out like the claustral ranges of a monastery.*

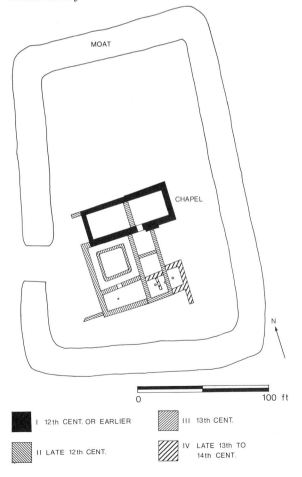

armies of laybrothers subject to monastic discipline. Excavation at Gorefields has indeed identified such a layout (**87**), and something similar is suggested by a twelfth-century two-storey range with a vaulted undercroft on the Rievaulx grange of Laskills. Field survey, however, indicates that this is not the norm and that the hundreds of granges that survive as earthworks or standing buildings are virtually indistinguishable from contemporary lay manors. Deserted sites commonly show an outer enclosure with barns and other farm buildings and an inner enclosure containing the principal domestic ranges.

The classic site, excavated in the mid 1960s, is the Knights Templar preceptory of South Witham, for all purposes a grange of the London Temple (**88**). South Witham had a short life, being founded between 1164 and 1185 and being abandoned before 1311, so it was not subjected to substantial redevelopment. All the same, excavation revealed several phases of building as the site grew with an expanding economy. Planned as a series of courts in similar fashion to a monastic precinct, the domestic ranges lay at the centre, more manorial in nature than monastic. To the north and west was a walled yard bordered by barns (1, 4, and 11) and animal houses (2, 3, and 6) with stone walls and thatched roofs. The yard also contained other service buildings including a metalworking shop (10). The site was chosen for its proximity to the River Witham, which was used to drive a corn-mill and to feed fishponds.

Mills were an important source of income to religious houses, for all tenants were obliged to use them, and corn-mills were a common feature of granges. Granges with access to rivers such as the Fountains grange of Bradley used their power for not only milling but also industrial processes. There, water-power was used for an important iron-working site which remains as a fine series of earthworks and extensive scatters of waste. Elaborate precautions were taken to ensure that Fountains controlled the River Colne both above and below this mill. An earlier site on the River Calder had been rejected because it was too close to the mill of Kirklees Priory upstream.

Water was not the only source of power available for milling. Many monasteries owned windmills, their sites betrayed by prominent mill-mounds or recorded in land-grants (**89**).

Barns are the most common of the grange

MOAT

CHAPEL

N

0   100 ft

I 12th CENT. OR EARLIER

II LATE 12th CENT.

III 13th CENT.

IV LATE 13th TO 14th CENT.

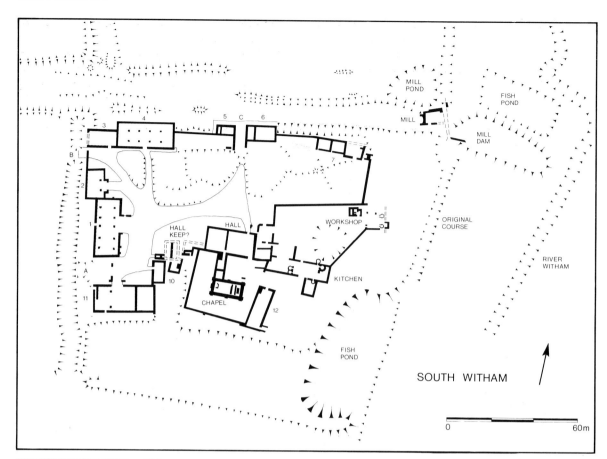

SOUTH WITHAM

0   60m

88 *(Top left.) The plan of South Witham recovered by total excavation demonstrates the most common layout of grange buildings and shows them to be as frequently altered as Outer Court structures (after Mayes).*

89 *(Bottom left.) A post-mill depicted on a cornice moulding from Rievaulx Abbey may well illustrate the most common form of windmill on the abbey's estates.*

90 *The earthworks of the Old Malton sheep-ranch on Levisham moor are a reminder that much of the evidence for monastic farming remains unexcavated and below ground (after Moorhouse).*

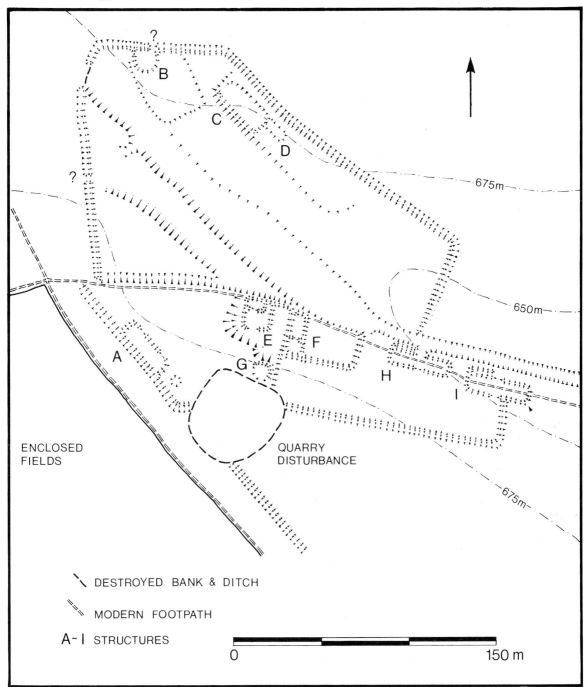

ENCLOSED
FIELDS

QUARRY
DISTURBANCE

DESTROYED BANK & DITCH

MODERN FOOTPATH

A~I STRUCTURES

0   150 m

buildings to survive, and few of these pre-date the thirteenth century. Whether or not this indicates that the building of granges was secondary to the initial establishment of a monastery is open to debate, though present indications are that permanent granges were often not provided until localized land-holdings were consolidated. This process was very much in evidence throughout the later twelfth and early thirteenth centuries. Thus the great barns on the Beaulieu granges of St Leonards and Great Coxwell were not built for more than half a century after the foundation of the monastery itself in 1204. The Great Coxwell barn survives almost as built, a building of the highest quality. Its framing with double braces demonstrates the internationalism of the Cistercians. In comparison, the Pershore Abbey grange of Leigh in Worcestershire retains the largest surviving cruck barn in England, built in the local vernacular tradition (**colour plate 10**).

Whilst the majority of granges practised a mixed economy, some were specialist in their function. Fountains Abbey for instance encouraged pottery production on its granges of Bradley, which also had extensive iron-workings and arable land, and Winksley, whilst Barlings Abbey maintained a fishery and smokehouses on the River Witham. Fountains and Rievaulx maintained large stud-farms in the Tees valley

to provide draught-horses for their widespread estates, and in the upland areas of England huge ranches for sheep (*bercaria*) and cattle (*vaccaria*) were common. One of the finest to survive is the Old Malton Priory bercary on Levisham moor (**90**), defined by a series of earthworks which suggest several phases of development. This ranch included pasture for 1000 sheep, 120 beasts, 20 mares with their foals, and 2 stallions. Excavation has yet to be used to demonstrate the way in which such granges were managed or what activities not evidenced by documents might have taken place on them. Like their parent houses they were occupied for three or more centuries, and in the later part of their life they were often tenanted rather than managed directly from the monastery. It is certain that their earthworks give an over-simplified view of what lies below.

Estimates vary as to the amount of land in monastic ownership throughout the Middle Ages, but a conservative estimate would be about one-seventh part of the land in use. Few areas had no monastic holdings, and in many parts of the country the development of granges had a dramatic effect on the medieval landscape, much of which still survives in spite of modern farming methods and four-and-a-half centuries of dispersal.

6

The suppression and after

In April 1536, there were still more than 800 abbeys and priories in England, largely with reduced communities, who between them enjoyed a cash income from their collected estates valued by the Commissioners of the *Valor Ecclesiasticus* at more than £160,000. This corporate wealth was far from equally spread, for Glastonbury had a net income in excess of £3000 whilst the poor nuns of Wilberfoss subsisted on an income of less than £40, and Wilberfoss was not the poorest house in England. Many houses were in debt or had few inmates, making the continuance of monastic life difficult. It is fair to assume that many of the smaller houses that had never accrued vast estates and that made up two-thirds of the total had neither fine buildings nor an unnecessarily worldly life style. The standard of spirituality they enjoyed varied immensely. In some cases it was virtually non-existent, in other houses discipline was good and beyond the reproach of the diocesan bishop.

On the whole, however, it could not be said that monastic life, with certain important exceptions, was in good order in the early years of Henry VIII. Cardinal Wolsey had begun to prune the dead wood, suppressing with papal authority no fewer than 29 houses such as Bayham and St Frideswide's in Oxford to fund new foundations, educational rather than monastic. Before him, John Alcock, Bishop of Ely, had secured papal consent to use St Radegund's Priory in Cambridge to house and endow Jesus College in 1497. With a growing secularization of society, monastic seclusion and rumoured good living off landed estates, a rift was growing between the common man and the cloistered religious.

The beginning of the end
The first actions in what was to become the

general suppression of the monasteries began as a genuine attempt at reform. Following the valuation of all church property in 1535, an Act was placed before Parliament in 1536 that suppressed all religious houses with small communities and an income of less than £200 a year where 'manifest sin, vicious, carnal, and abominable living' was daily practised. The displaced monks and nuns, canons and canonesses, could either be transferred to 'divers and great solemn monasteries of this realm wherein, thanks be to God, religion is right well kept and observed', or to take 'capacities' and leave their cloisters. The lands and buildings that they left were to become the property of the state, to be used for other, more productive purposes. The Parliament which passed the Act contained no fewer than 30 abbots and priors whose own wealthy houses were not included. Poor friaries were specifically not included in the act, and provision was made for exemptions. The number of religious who chose to remain within the cloister effectively meant that some of the poorer houses and all those of the Gilbertines and small cells dependant on larger houses had to be retained to house them. In all, less than one-third of the total were suppressed. The process of closure and asset-stripping took place throughout the spring and summer of 1536 and established a process which was to become highly organized over the following years. The Court of Augmentations was established to deal with the revenues created as contents were sold, lands were leased, and staff paid off in the course of dismantling many centuries of monastic life.

In spite of the care taken by the government to make the case for reform, the suppression of houses known for their piety and hospitality caused hostility, particularly in the north, contributing to a popular rebellion, the 'Pilgrimage of Grace' in October 1536. The 'Pilgrims' were not entirely motivated by the loss of their monasteries, but the return of the monks and nuns to their empty cloisters rapidly became their aim, much to the concern of the new tenants and the King himself. The rebels in Yorkshire and Lincolnshire coerced leading chuchmen – the Abbots of Jervaulx, Whalley, Kirkstead, and Barlings, together with the Prior of Bridlington and an ex-Abbot of Fountains – to support their cause, and when the revolt collapsed they were tried as traitors,

executed, and their estates seized by the crown. In the case of the abbots and priors, this was taken to mean their wealthy monasteries, which fell in 1537 not to the Court of Augmentations but to the King himself. Whilst the smaller

91 *Randal Holmes' plan of Chester cathedral made before 1626 shows most of the buildings associated with St Werbergh's Abbey which survived to serve the dean and chapter of the new foundation.*

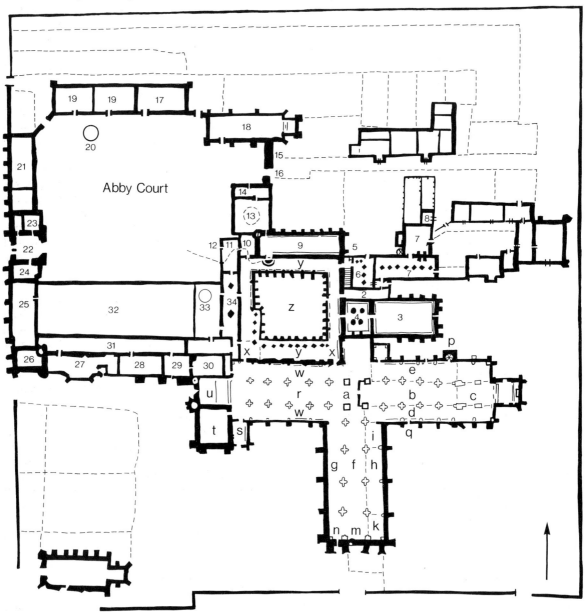

monasteries suppressed in 1536 had brought small profits to the crown, the pickings from these wealthy houses were far greater and showed what could be gained from the major abbeys. The roof leads alone of Jervaulx and Kirkstead were valued at more than £1000, and at Bridlington only a little less. All the houses had extensive and valuable estates and were an obvious source of profit to the Crown.

Following on from these seizures by attainder, the government's approach to the monasteries rapidly changed, and what had begun as a genuine attempt at reform now became a systematic attempt to rid the country of all monks and nuns. This time, persuasion was used, beginning with the abbey of Furness. Several of the monks there had sided with the rebels, but this could not be used as a reason to seize the house, one which in 1536 had been considered to be a place where religion was well kept. The abbot, when approached by the suppression commissioners immediately surrendered his house to the King, beginning a process which was only ratified by Act of Parliament in 1538, and which continued until the last surviving house at Waltham was suppressed in March 1540.

Monasteries into cathedrals

The dissolution of the monasteries was the first significant act in the restructuring of the English church. Its first affect was the re-establishment of those cathedral-priories that had been served by Benedictine monks. The prior was replaced by a dean and the monks by a chapter of canons, in many cases the previous monks. In this way, the cathedrals of Canterbury, Durham, Worcester, Winchester, Rochester, Ely, Norwich and Carlisle were recreated out of existing buildings, altered to suit the needs of a secular clergy who no longer lived a common life. Six other monasteries were retained to increase the number of cathedral churches – Westminster, Bristol, Oxford, Gloucester, Peterborough and Chester (91) ensuring the preservation of not only their churches but also a proportion of the other buildings required by the new chapter. Westminster was later reduced to the status of a collegiate church but retained many of its buildings.

One site initially chosen to be one of these cathedrals of the New Foundation was Fountains Abbey, where the church and cloister ranges were 'mothballed' for a short period before the scheme was abandoned. This short-lived stay of execution might have kept the buildings intact but did not mean that no damage was done. Excavation by Walbran in the 1850s indicated that many graves had been looted, although he was unable to ascertain when this had happened. The excavation in 1979 of the grave in the south transept of brother John Rypon (92) who died in 1524 identified graphically the sequence of events which must have happened whilst the church was still in royal hands. The grave slab had been lifted and broken, and the upper half of the grave cut dug out, disturbing the body, which was still at least partially articulated, to retrieve the mortuary chalice and paten that had been buried with the priest. The remains of John Rypon were then thrown back into the grave with no attempt to replace them correctly, and the grave refilled. This in itself is hardly remarkable, but the next occurrence is. The grave slab was carefully relaid, though part of it had been thrown into the grave fill, and missing areas were made up with plaster which was not apparent until excavation. Such a restoration can only have taken place within the context of the church being in the care of the suppression commissioners and would imply that the looting, for once at least, was unauthorized.

The exploitation of monastic sites

The sites which were not retained for church use were normally sold to laymen, and indeed many patrons sought to purchase the houses their families had supported for generations. Though they were not always successful, there are many cases in which the provider became the despoiler, converting newly-acquired buildings and lands to capital in order to fund his purchase. It was a requirement of sale, following the experience of the Pilgrimage of Grace where monks had been reinstated in their suppressed houses, that the commissioners, or failing them the new owner, should 'pull down to the ground all the walls of the churches, stepulls, cloysters, fraterys, dorters, chapter howsys etc', though this did not always happen. The portions of the church that were parochial were by and large retained, though they might have been stripped of their contents and of their lead roofs, and had to be purchased from the crown if they were to continue. In this way,

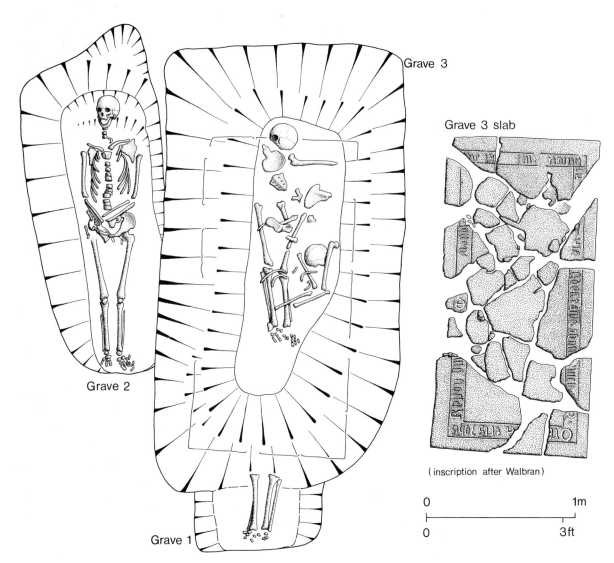

Grave 3

Grave 3 slab

(inscription after Walbran)

| 0 | | 1m |
| 0 | | 3ft |

Grave 2

Grave 1

92 *The grave of brother John Rypon in the south transept of Fountains Abbey had been robbed and restored in 1539.*

the naves of Bridlington, Wymondham, Bolton, Malmesbury, Leominster, Binham and Bourne survived the wreck, and on a lesser scale the north nave aisle at Crowland was preserved. It was not just the parochial nave that survived; at Swine it was the nuns' church that the parish sought to acquire, whilst at Boxgrove Priory it was the presence of the de la Warre tombs in the presbytery that ensured that the late patron and new owner retained that part of the church in favour of the smaller parochial nave. More

rarely, whole churches were purchased for parish use – at Christchurch and Romsey in Hampshire, Dorchester in Oxfordshire, Selby in Yorkshire and Hexham in Northumberland.

These however were the exceptions. The degree of destruction was variable. Many churches were simply unroofed and left to the elements, but others were thoroughly demolished, even to the removal of their foundations. At Jervaulx and Bardney (see **9**), Hailes and Norton, the churches were levelled soon after their closure, partly to comply with the condition of purchase and partly to provide building materials for houses created within the cloister ranges. At Lewes Priory, for which contemporary accounts survive, one Giovanni

Portarini and a gang of 25 Italian engineers working for Thomas Cromwell were employed to level the church quickly using mines and gunpowder. In this way the great Cluniac church of St Pancras with its high steeple and vaults 28 m (93 ft) above its pavements was reduced to low walling in less than four weeks in March and April 1538 before Cromwell's son Gregory took possession of the site. The cost of such demolition was one of the principal reasons for the policy of total destruction not being carried out. In Lincolnshire, a county where the level of destruction was greater than most, John Freeman, who was charged with the task of demolition, estimated that it could be done only at a cost of more than £1000 and was content simply to make the churches unusable and let stone robbers do the rest.

There were, however, cases where specific monasteries were earmarked to provide stone for royal works. Meaux Abbey, for instance, was largely demolished to provide stone for the King's new fortifications at Hull, and excavation there on the site of Henry VIII's citadel and its flanking walls has produced clear evidence of worked medieval stone in the core of the surviving structure. Similarly, the transepts and presbytery of Bridlington Priory were sacrificed for the building of a new quay in the harbour there that fell into royal hands in 1537 along with the priory itself.

There are many documented cases of monastic buildings being broken up, but one of the most instructive cases is that of Rievaulx Abbey and its home estates purchased by its 'founder' or patron, the Earl of Rutland, in 1538. There, no demolition had begun, and the site came intact to its new owner, though the crown had retained the bells, the lead from the roofs of the church, chapter-house, dormitory, refectory, kitchen, cloister, charnel chapel and gate-house, together with the timber of the cloister roofs to burn it down. There was to be no orgy of destruction, and the dismantling of the site was carried out in such a way as to maximize profit. First, the King's lead was cast down into 'sows' of half a fother, perhaps in the cloister garth. Four pigs, each weighing approximately nine hundredweights (half a short ton) and marked with the crowned Tudor rose to prove its ownership (93), were found below tons of fallen masonry at the west end of the nave, lost when the twelfth century building collapsed of its own accord. Although the furnaces to melt

the lead have yet to be found, they are well evidenced by excavation at Hailes, Croxden, Bordesley, Muchelney, Sopwell, Durham, Pontefract, the Franciscan church in Northampton, and Monk Bretton. From Walbran's description of the stall-bases at Fountains, they must have been in the choir area there. Next, the screenwork in the church was sold, followed by the timber roof and its lead covering of the west range to tenants of the Earl who had previously been tenants of the abbey. Then, the window glass was to be taken out and sorted, the best to be kept, the second quality to be sold in panels, the poorest to be taken from its leads which were then to be melted down. The thousands of pieces of glass recovered by excavation must represent only what was felt to be worthless in 1538/9. Even the scrap iron was to be sorted and sold before it rusted and lost value, down to the nails that fixed the boarding below the lead on the roofs. Such was the desire to maximize the profits that even 'the lede of the joyntes of the pyllers and other placys, of as much as is defasyd of the ppremysses there, now is fastenyd within stonys not lose' was sold speculatively. To judge from the vast quantities of lead and iron left among the heaps of demolition rubble that Peers removed in the 1920s, the interest in recovering the total value of the scrap was soon forgotten.

The destruction at Rievaulx, as on so many other sites, was not complete, and useful buildings were retained undamaged. Unwanted buildings were simply made unusable and slowed quarried, the intention being that the monasteries could not be easily restored. To conform with the condition of purchase, the piers that supported the clerestory of the chapter-house (94) and the vault of the east range were cut to take wedges that were driven in until the monolithic shafts cracked and could be pulled out thus bringing down the superstructure, which was left where it fell. Iron wedges and sledge-hammers were found amongst the fallen debris.

The church itself did not need this treatment. The steeple on the central tower had already fallen before the suppression and was lying on the floor of the south transept, and the nave actually collapsed in the course of its being dismantled. Though the Earl had given instructions that the fine west window, perhaps only 30 years old, should be removed and stored in his castle at Helmsley, glass, iron, and

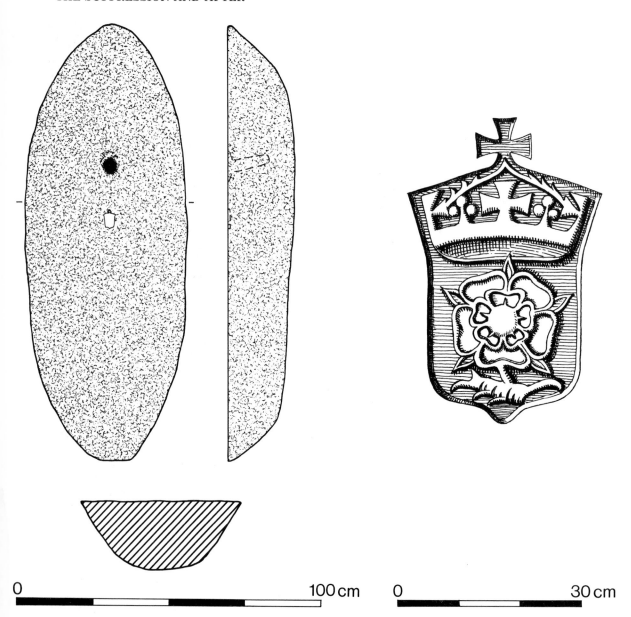

0   **100 cm**   0   **30 cm**

93 *One of the four half-fothers of lead from the spoliation of Rievaulx Abbey marked with the king's badge (G. Dunning).*

stonework complete, the masonry of the window was found in the collapsed debris of the west end of the nave in 1920.

The survival of individual buildings
Provision was however made to save something from the destruction. No fewer than 18 tenanted buildings remained untouched within the precinct at Rievaulx, though the church and cloister ranges were dismantled in 1539. These were to form the nucleus of the village that succeeded the abbey and was largely built from its remains. In addition, the three abbey mills, one for corn, a fulling mill, and a water-powered smithy, remained a valuable asset. By far the greatest survivor, though, was the abbot's house (**95**), retained as a suitable house for a tenant or 'farmer' (not necessarily employed in agriculture). It was less than 40 years old, of

94 *The broken monolithic piers that supported the superstructure of the chapter-house at Rievaulx Abbey still bear marks of the wedges used to bring them down in 1538.*

sound construction, and retained its lead and slate roofs, floors, doors and wainscot panelling. The hall even retained its tiled floor and furniture. A substantial house, with its hall and chambers above cellarage, the great chamber over a fine parlour, together with a chapel, a private dining chamber, and a substantial kitchen, it provided better domestic accommodation than the Earl's castle of Helmsley 3 km (2 miles) away and survived until it was replaced by a large farmhouse in the eighteenth century. This house itself survived until the 1950s when it was finally demolished.

Sound buildings were in any case saleable, and where possible they were spared. In Gloucester, the remarkable survival of the Dominican priory was the result of the extensive reuse of its buildings. The site was sold intact to Alderman Thomas Bell, who converted the church into a grand mansion, Bell's Place, and the cloister ranges into a weaving factory, ensuring their survival to the present day. The suppression commissioners were charged with selling the movables of any monastery they closed, and the buildings that remained to be sold off must have been stripped bare. The interpretation of movable objects was broad, including not simply the furniture and household goods but also paving stones, floor tiles, grave stones, and any iron and lead work that could be easily removed. This process has been graphically demonstrated in the north range of the lesser cloister of the Dominican priory at Beverley (**96**). Though the building was not finally taken down until the seventeenth century, its latest medieval floor retained the evidence of the suppressors at work. Discarded window glass was scattered throughout the building, and the window leads recovered had been melted down in bowl hearths cut into the floors of each room. Fuel for melting down the lead and the brick to line one of the hearths had been taken from internal partitions that had been stripped out for the purpose. Lead water pipes were systematically removed, and

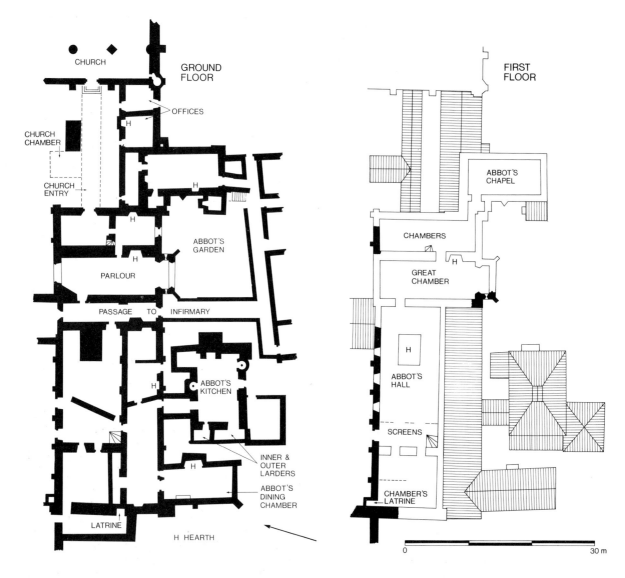

95 *The plan of the abbot's house at Rievaulx can be reconstructed from surviving fragments and from its descriptions in a series of contemporary surveys and inventories.*

even the lead lining of the gulley that took water from the cloister alley roof was recovered. Scoops in the floors of both principal rooms seem to have been used for casting the lead into small ingots, and considerable quantities of lead runlets and dross from the melting process were spread about the building. On the completion of this work, the bowl hearths were carefully plugged and the scrapes in the floor filled up, leaving the building a useable shell once more.

Monasteries into mansions

Cloister ranges might easily be converted into a house for the new owner with little effort. In the most basic cases the president's lodging, and in some cases the guest accommodation, survived little altered well into the post-medieval period. At Norton and Hailes, Bardney and Waverley, this has been demonstrated by excavation and eighteenth-century illustrations (**97**) to be in the west cloister range, with all the unwanted buildings swept away and buried beneath gardens. In the case of Hailes,

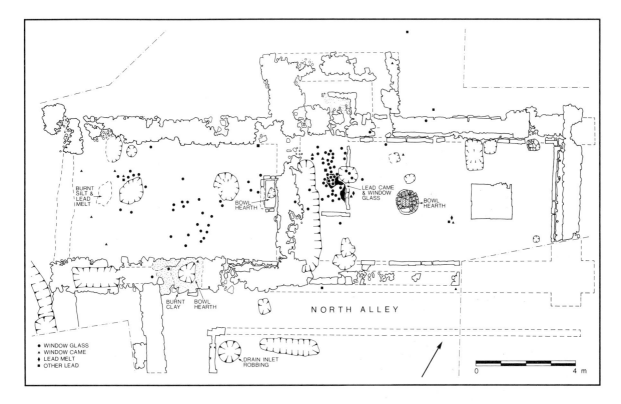

BURNT
SILT &
LEAD
MELT

BOWL
HEARTH

LEAD CAME
& WINDOW
GLASS

BOWL
HEARTH

BURNT   BOWL
CLAY   HEARTH

NORTH ALLEY

● WINDOW GLASS
▲ WINDOW CAME
♦ LEAD MELT
■ OTHER LEAD

DRAIN INLET
ROBBING

0   4 m

96 *The north range of the lesser cloister at Dominican Friary in Beverley retained traces of small-scale spoliation by the suppression commissioners though the building itself was to survive into the seventeenth century (after Foreman).*

Bardney and Waverley, the cloister walls themselves were retained to enclose a garden, a continuing use of the garth. On the last two sites the medieval doors in the surviving walls retained evidence of their blockings when they were excavated. In many ways, the cloister garth at Norton was much more interesting archaeologically for it contained a rubbish dump associated with the post-suppression house.

Sadly, the archaeology of post-suppression houses on monastic sites has been largely ignored and in many cases simply swept away to reveal the underlying medieval structure. One important exception is the house begun but never completed on the site of the small Benedictine nunnery at Sopwell by Sir Richard Lee in the 1550s (**98**). Lee began by building a small courtyard house around the nuns' cloister, with his hall on the site of their church and the cloister garth laid out as a cobbled yard surrounded by ranges. This plan was then abandoned, and a much larger double courtyard house laid out over the levelled remains of the first building and not reflecting the medieval layout of the site at all but respecting its orientation. The new building was never completed, probably because of the death of its builder in 1575. Its development might perhaps be paralleled by great post-medieval houses like Woburn Abbey which occupy medieval monastic sites and must have developed from them by degrees.

A significant number of monastic buildings survive because they were reused in this way, either great houses, such as those built by the abbots of Battle or Ford and the prior of Watton, that required little alteration to make them suitable residences for new owners of rank, or buildings of manorial status like the west range of Lanercost Priory, or the refectories of Horsham St Faith or Syningthwaite which required little work to turn them into simple houses.

Occasionally, the greater part of the claustral nucleus was retained to form a major house.

THE EAST VIEW OF HALES ABBY, IN THE COUNTY OF GLOUCESTER.

To the R.^t Honble **THOMAS TRACY** Visc.^t & Baron Tracy of *RATHCOOLE in the County of Dublin, &c.* Lord of these Remains. This Prospect is humbly inscrib'd by Y.^r Lordsp.^s most Obed.^t Serv.^{ts} Saml & Nathl Buck.

THIS ABBY was built by Richard Plantagenet 2.^d Son of K. John and Brother to K. Hen. 3. Earl of Cornwal & King of the Romans, pursuant to a Vow he had made when in extreme Danger at Sea, he placed in it Cistercian Monks and dedicated it to St Mary & all Saints. It was consecrated with unusual great Pomp in the Presence of the King, Queen a great number of the Nobility and 300 Knights, by Walter Cantilupe, Bishop of Worcester & thirteen other Bishops assisting. S. & N. Buck del. et sc. 1732.

97 *The abbot's house in the west cloister range of Hailes Abbey, illustrated by Samuel Buck in the early eighteenth century, formed the basis of a post-suppression house built by the Tracys. The church, with its shrine of the Holy Blood, is buried beneath the gardens.*

At Netley Abbey, which was acquired by Sir William Paulet, later Marquis of Winchester, the only cloister building to be demolished was the refectory which was replaced by a modest gatehouse. The cloister became a courtyard with a central fountain, the transepts and nave became the hall and kitchen, the presbytery became the chapel, and the east and west ranges were partitioned to form a series of private apartments. So little work was required to effect this change of use that the only clues surviving today are inserted windows. Excavation in 1860 resulted in the unfortunate removal of many post-suppression walls and the bases of three great kitchen fireplaces in the nave to 'reveal better its peculiarities as an ecclesiastical edifice'. This was a sad loss because the Paulet house, which survived in use until 1790, would have told us a great deal about the method of conversion from monastery to mansion.

At another Hampshire site, sufficient fabric and a remarkable series of contemporary documents survive to demonstrate the process, though on a more destructive scale. Thomas Wriothesley, a close associate of Cromwell, petitioned for the site of Titchfield Abbey, which was suppressed on 18 December 1537. Four days later he was advised by the suppression commissioners who continued to act as his agents that the cost of conversion of the monastic buildings to a suitable house would be in excess of £200. On 30 December he was finally granted the site, and three days later the commissioners advised him of their scheme to create a mansion fit 'for the Kings grace to bate & for any baron to kepe his hospitalite in'. Such speedy action was consistent with the commissioners' instructions to prevent the return of the canons who had been dispossessed. They were also keen to demolish the church with the exception of the north transept to ensure that the abbey was effectively defaced, but Wriothesley would have none of this.

Although the work of conversion began immediately there were constant changes to the plan between January and April 1538. Initially it had been planned to put the hall on the first floor of the east range, but the final scheme placed it more sensibly in the old refectory, which was largely rebuilt and provided with a porch into the cloister garth which

98 *Excavation of the ruinous sixteenth century house on the site of Sopwell Priory has revealed not one but two post-suppression houses, the first built around the nuns' cloister, the second ignoring it (after Johnson).*

became a courtyard with a central fountain. The great chamber and parlour were then placed in the east range above cellarage and a chapel which seems to have occupied the chapter-house, whilst servants' quarters were contrived within the west range, which was extensively rebuilt. Arguments continued

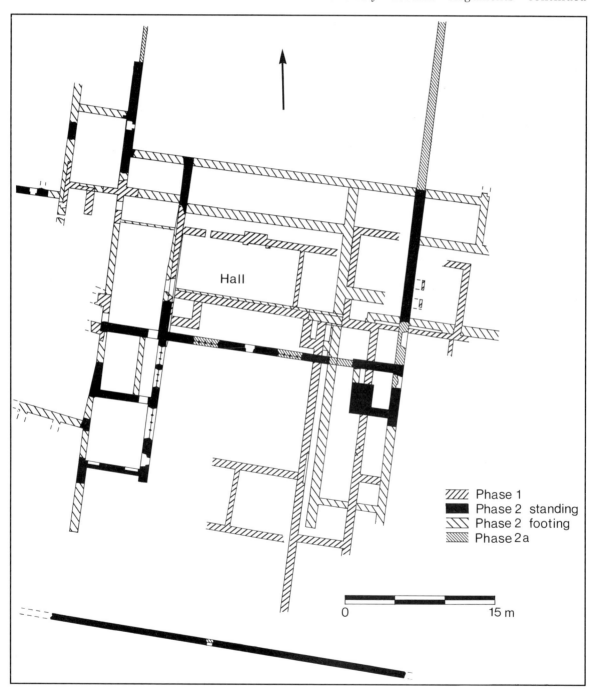

Hall

Phase 1
Phase 2 standing
Phase 2 footing
Phase 2a

0   15 m

99 *The gatehouse range at Wriothesley's Place House at Titchfield reuses the nave of the thirteenth-century priory.*

throughout the summer about the refitting of the church. Wriothesley finally accepted that the crossing tower and south transept should be demolished, though the presbytery and crossing were to form the shell of three lodgings. The final phase of building (**99**) was the gatehouse range that closed the south side of the courtyard, constructed from the nave of the abbey church through which a striking gatehouse with octagonal turrets was driven. Sadly all but the gatehouse range was demolished in 1781, though what survives shows that the conversion work was skilfully contrived and that it would have been difficult to tell that the sixteenth century mansion of Place House was for the most part a Premonstratensian abbey of the thirteenth century. The house was finished by 1542 when its owner sought the royal

pardon for crenellating it without licence, almost certainly because of the new gatehouse, and when John Leland wrote in his Itinerary that 'Mr Wriothesley hath builded a right stately house embateled and having a goodely gate and a conducte (conduit) casteled in the middle of the court of it, yn the very same place where the late Monasterie of Premonstratenses stoode, caullyd Tichfelde'. It is only with its ruin that the origins of the site have become truly apparent.

Wholesale conversion was not a rare occurrence. At Lacock for instance Sir William Sharington's new house made use of the Augustinian canoness' cloister ranges and inner court but required the demolition of their

100 *The earthworks of Stainfield, a small Benedictine nunnery, detail several phases of settlement, the latest of which is a post-medieval park associated with Stainfield Hall. No monastic buildings survive (P. Everson/RCHM).*

Park Cottages

Stainfield Beck

e

d

c

St Andrew's Church

Stainfield Hall

k

a

b

h

i

j

g

f

Top Houses

Metres
0   100   200

0   600
Feet

church, very much on the same model as Newstead Priory where only the south aisle of the nave and south transept were included in the house created at the suppression. At Mottisfont Priory and Buckland Abbey, it was the church that formed the basis of a house, though the greater part of the remaining monastic buildings were demolished. Where the church and cloister buildings were swept away or remodelled it was still common to retain the gatehouse to serve new buildings, explaining the survival of the great gates of Thornton Abbey, and St Osyth's Priory. In some cases, it was the gatehouse itself which became a house, with fine surviving examples at Beaulieu, Butley, Kirkstall and Bolton.

Although the method of converting the main monastic buildings into new houses is well established, little attention has ever been paid to other changes brought about within the remainder of the precinct. At Thornholme Priory, where substantial outlying areas have been excavated, it was possible to demonstrate that most of the service buildings were thoroughly demolished immediately after the suppression, to the extent that virtually all their masonry was removed (see **81**), though the same destruction was not apparent in the cloister ranges and the gatehouse had not been demolished until the nineteenth century.

At Stainfield Priory, the earthworks of the precinct (**100**) show without doubt that they were modified after the suppression to serve as the park for Stainfield Hall, giving the lie to the assumption that all earthworks on monastic sites need be medieval. In some cases, the post-suppression modification of the landscape was just as drastic as that caused by the building of the monasteries in the first place. In the case of Southwick Priory, the extent of the precinct is completely obscured by the earthworks that defined the building and garden terraces of a great seventeenth-century house which has been as effectively demolished as the priory buildings themselves.

Ruins in the landscape

Those monastic sites that were not reused as houses were simply abandoned or served as quarries, and the survival of their ruins has been very much a matter of luck. At Whitby, the abbot's house survived as a residence, but the church was simply stripped of its roof, windows and bells and left to serve as a sea-mark. Its subsequent fate is indicative of how

101 *Buck's engraving of Whitby Abbey, taken from a drawing of 1711, shows the masonry of the church and chapter-house to be largely intact.*

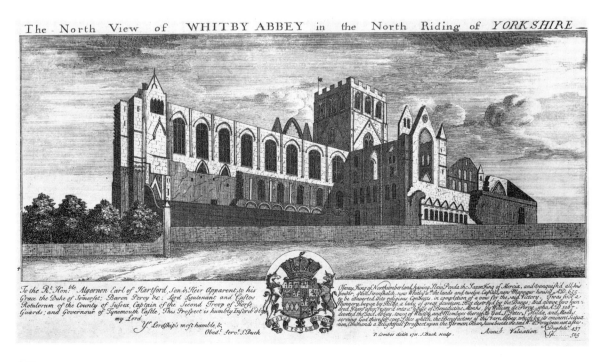

The North View of WHITBY ABBEY in the North Riding of YORKSHIRE

the simple forces of nature could be just as destructive as the suppression commissioners. It is fortunate indeed that the ruins of the church at Whitby have been so well recorded in the past, for the losses have been dramatic. The earliest known record was engraved by Samuel Buck in the first quarter of the eighteenth century (**101**) and shows the thirteenth- and fourteenth-century church tolerably complete together with the greater part of the chapter-house. Though the major windows appear to have lost their tracery, the gables remain intact as do a number of pinnacles. Whilst Buck's engravings cannot be regarded as a totally accurate record – he does for instance claim that his view is taken from the north whilst it is in fact taken from the south-west, and he fails to show the surviving remains of the abbot's house – later drawings of a much better quality do show a number of features recorded by Buck that no longer survive, confirming the broad outlines of his record.

Another engraving of 1789 after Gibson (**102**) shows a very different state of affairs. Two-and-a-half centuries of neglect and the harsh climate of the Whitby headland had caused major falls of masonry. The arcades and clerestory of the nave had fallen in 1762, to be followed by the south transept the following year, their tumbled remains lying where they had fallen. While the ruins were the subject of Romantic curiosity, as is evident from the group in the foreground, no attempt was made to repair them for the greater part of the west front was to fall in 1794, a victim of continuing decay. The Gibson drawing is extremely useful because of its great attention to detail, evidencing the date of masonry that no longer survives. The tower, which remains intact to the string-course below its parapet, was built in the fourteenth century and was contemporary with the completion of the nave, although it stands above a crossing of thirteenth-century date (see **12**). On its west face are two weatherings that

102 *Gibson's drawing of Whitby in 1789, after the fall of the nave and south transept, but before the loss of the crossing tower.*

mark the position of roofs. The lower one, just above the crossing arch, must have been the temporary roof of an uncompleted nave of thirteenth-century date, the upper one is that of the fourteenth-century nave that collapsed in 1762. The west window, a Perpendicular window of eight transomed lights to judge from its stubs, was an insertion of the fifteenth century, clear evidence that the fourteenth-century nave was altered and improved, though the scale of this work is no longer apparent.

When the ruins of Whitby Abbey were taken into the care of the Office of Works in 1920, they were much less extensive than the ruins shown in the Gibson drawing (**103**). The crossing tower had fallen on 25 June 1830, and part of the presbytery fell during a storm in 1839. In comparison shelling by the German navy on 16 December 1914 did little serious damage to the ruins. Without intentional demolition or the depredations of stone robbers more than half the abbey church had simply collapsed before any attempt was made to halt the decay and preserve what remained for posterity. The

removal of hundreds of tons of fallen masonry in the early 1920s has done something to recover the plan and elevation of what was a remarkable building (**104**), but it cannot restore what was lost through three-and-a-half centuries of neglect. The course of events seen at Whitby was by no means unique. The north-west or Ethelbert tower at St Augustine's Abbey in Canterbury for instance fell in 1822. Although the repair of many of the most important monastic ruins from the late nineteenth century has ensured that the loss of fabric is largely a thing of the past there are still sites which continue to decay. One tragic loss of the last decade has been the crossing tower of Maxstoke Priory, and without proper attention other monastic sites remain at risk.

103 *In 1840, only the north wall of the nave, the north transept and the presbytery remained standing, obscured by great heaps of fallen masonry.*

104 *Following the clearance of the site in the 1920s, romantic ruin has given way to didactic display and permanent preservation.*

Romantic ruins and eighteenth-century parks

It was the image of ruin and natural decay that brought the best preserved of our abbeys and priories to the attention of their owners in the eighteenth and early nineteenth centuries. What had ceased to be strictly practical now became art to be appreciated. A good abbey ruin was a fine feature for a gentleman's park. In the eighteenth-century interpretation of the picturesque a real ruin was infinitely preferable to a manufactured one, and several of the northern abbeys were particularly suited to this use. The finest of all monastic ruins, those of the great Cistercian abbey of Fountains, lay in the valley of the River Skell to the west of the gardens created at Studley Royal by John Aislabie, the Chancellor of the Exchequer disgraced by the South Sea Bubble scandal of 1720. Though he was unable to purchase the

site, his design was to use the ruins as a vista at the west end of his water-gardens (**colour plate 4**), for according to the traveller Arthur Young 'ruins generally appear best at a distance'. His son acquired the Fountains estate in 1768, incorporating the ruins in an extension of his father's gardens which was conceived not in the classical formality of his father's designs but in the picturesque romantic style which 'Capability' Brown was bringing to Roche at about the same time. Undoubtedly, it was the bringing of the ruins into the gardens that ensured their future well-being, though at the time this was questioned.

The ruins were not quite to William Aislabie's taste so they were improved, not simply by selective demolition but by the addition of new features. Gilpin, who visited in 1772 was not at all impressed by Aislabie's treatment of the ruins:

A few fragments scattered about the body of a ruin are proper and picturesque. They are proper because they account for what is defaced; and they are picturesque, because they unite the principal parts with the ground in which union the beauty of composition in a good measure depends. But here they are thought rough and unsightly, and fell a sacrifice to neatness... In the room of these detached parts, which are proper and picturesque embellishments of the scene, a gaudy temple is erected, and other trumpery wholly foreign to it. But not only the scene is defaced, and the *outworks of the ruin* violently torn away; *the main body of the ruin itself* is at this very time under the alarming hand of decoration. When the present proprietor made his purchase, he found the whole mass of ruins – the Cloisters, the Abbey Church, and the Hall – choked with rubbish. The first work therefore was to clear and open. And something in this way might have been done with propriety, for we see ruins sometimes so choked that no view of them can be obtained... But the restoration of parts is not enough: ornaments must be added, and such incongruous ornament, as disgrace the scene are disgracing also the monastery. The monks' garden is turned into a trim parterre and planted with flowering shrubs; a view is opened through the great window to some ridiculous I know not what (Anne Bolein I think they call it) that is planted in the valley; and in the central part of the abbey, a circular pedestal is raised out of fragments of the old pavement, on which is erected a mutilated heathen statue!

Whilst Gilpin's complaints were largely a matter of taste, it is obvious that Aislabie did considerable damage to the archaeology and structure of the site. He swept away the remains of the elegant late-twelfth-century cloister arcades, and removed the arcades from the presbytery. He also spread fallen masonry about the site to establish levels for his all-pervading lawns, removing architectural detail from its original context.

If this was the negative side of Aislabie's contribution to Fountains Abbey, there was a positive element which far outweighed the damage done. Aislabie, his daughter Mrs Allanson and her niece Mrs Lawrence conducted a long-term campaign of repair and resetting of fallen masonry. It was Mrs Allanson who permitted the excavation of the chapter-house by John Martin, and Mrs Lawrence who first allowed Richard Walbran to excavate in the church. Her successor, the Earl de Grey, in his turn was responsible for the clearance of the ruins to the state in which they can be seen today. He was also responsible for opening the ruins to the public and for sponsoring the recording of the site by J. A. Reeve. The worst excesses that Gilpin complained of were effectively reversed as scholarly interests came to influence the noble owners.

The monastic legacy

Without doubt it was the growing interest in monastic sites throughout the nineteenth century described in Chapter 1 that led to the survival of so many sites. Many others have not survived above ground but remain a future reserve of buried knowledge. Their excavation and the continuing study and analysis of those buildings which survive above ground, will continue the growth of our knowledge and interpretation of our monastic past. Though considerable progress has been made, our knowledge of monastic life in medieval England remains imperfect and there are many avenues of research that remain to be followed up. One of the most important is, quite simply, to discover what happened to our monasteries and their estates after they ceased to be corporations of piety and workshops of prayer.

Gazetteer

This gazetteer lists all those sites mentioned in the text where there is actually something to see, together with the modern county, the order of monks, nuns, canons, canonesses or friars who lived there, and a brief description of what remains to be seen. Monasteries that became cathedrals are not included; they are identified in Chapter 6 and are sufficiently well known and accessible not to warrant inclusion. Those sites marked with an asterisk are at least partially in the care of English Heritage and are open to the public. Others are still in use by the church and are usually accessible. Many more are privately owned and not all of these are open to the public. Those on farm-land can normally be visited with the permission of the land-owner or tenant.

* Abbotsbury Abbey (Dorset), Benedictine monks. The eastern gable of one of the conventual buildings survives, together with the remains of the abbey gatehouse, the mill (now a private house), and precinct barn.

Alnwick Abbey (Northumberland), Premonstratensian canons. The gatehouse is all that remains above ground.

Bardney Abbey (Lincs.), Benedictine monks. Clear traces of the church, cloister ranges and inner court, backfilled but remaining as earthworks, together with less prominent earthworks of the outer court and precinct wall.

Barlings Abbey (Lincs.), Premonstratensian canons. Fine earthworks of the whole precinct with a surviving fragment of the church.

* Battle Abbey (Sussex), Benedictine monks. The church and chapter-house survive as low walling (the greater part of the church remaining buried), but the east and west ranges of the cloister buildings remain. The west range, now a private school, comprises the abbot's house and is for the most part medieval. To the south-west of the cloister buildings is the basement of the monastic guest-house. The site is partially enclosed by a well-preserved precinct wall with a fine gatehouse of twelfth to fourteenth century date.

*Bayham Abbey (Sussex), Premonstratensian canons. The ruins of the church, cloister buildings and gatehouse remain in an early-nineteenth-century landscape associated with an important Gothick mansion. This landscape contains elements of the monastic precinct.

Beaulieu Abbey (Hants.), Cistercian monks. Fragmentary ruins of the abbey church and east cloister range, though the refectory (now the parish church) and west range survive intact, as does the inner gatehouse incorporated in a post-suppression mansion. Elements of the precinct survive within parkland.

*Binham Priory (Norfolk), Benedictine monks. The nave of the church remains in use, though the transepts, presbytery and cloister buildings exist only as ruins. Much of the precinct can still be traced from surviving earthworks.

Birkenhead Priory (Greater Manchester), Benedictine monks. Remains of the cloister ranges.

Bolton Priory (North Yorks.), Augustinian canons. The nave of the church remains in use, though the eastern parts are roofless. The cloister buildings are represented only by low walling. The precinct, which is still partly enclosed by a precinct wall with a gatehouse (now incorporated within a post-suppression house) can still be traced as earthworks.

Bordesley Abbey (Hereford and Worcester), Cistercian monks. Essentially an earthwork site representing the whole of the monastic precinct. A long-term research excavation continues which has already exposed the eastern parts of the church, the gate-chapel and an industrial site.

Bourne Abbey (Lincs.), Augustinian canons. The nave of the priory church remains in parish use.

*** Boxgrove Priory** (Sussex), Benedictine monks. The eastern parts of the church survive intact and in use, together with the ruins of the nave, chapter-house and a detached building that is perhaps a combined infirmary and president's lodging.

Bradenstoke Priory (Wilts.), Augustinian canons. The west range of the cloister survives, containing the prior's lodging converted to a post-suppression house. The precinct is well defined by surviving earthworks and contains a fine medieval barn.

Bridlington Priory (Humberside), Augustinian canons. The parochial nave of the church remains in use with slight traces of the west cloister range and fragments of the cloister arcade (re-erected in the church). The gate-house, altered in the post-suppression period, is now a museum.

Buckland Abbey (Devon), Cistercian monks. The church remains, converted to a post-suppression mansion.

*** Bury St Edmunds** (Suffolk), Benedictine monks. Substantial ruins of the abbey church and its claustral ranges in the setting of a public park and cemetery which comprises the whole of the precinct. The precinct wall with two gatehouses and two parochial churches (one now the cathedral) survives largely intact.

*** Byland Abbey** (North Yorks.), Cistercian monks. The extensive ruins of the church (with extensive remains of its tiled floors) and cloister buildings survive within the well-preserved earthworks of the precinct which demonstrate the complexity of water-management on a difficult site. A fragment of the inner gatehouse survives to the north of College Farm. Site Museum with an exceptional display of architectural detail.

*** Canterbury, St Augustine's Abbey** (Kent), Benedictine monks. Ruins of both the Saxon and Norman abbey churches remain visible, together with parts of the east, north and west cloister ranges. Part of the west range and the Inner Court, which contained the abbot's lodging and Henry VIII's post-suppression house, was incorporated in William Butterfield's St Augustine's College in 1848, now used by the King's School.

Christchurch Priory (Dorset), Augustinian canons. The church remains intact, converted to parochial use at the suppression.

*** Creake Abbey** (Norfolk), Augustinian canons. The ruins of the eastern parts of the church remain, together with a post-suppression house within the south cloister range.

Crowland Abbey (Lincs.), Benedictine monks. The north aisle of the nave remains in use as the parish church, and the remainder of the nave which retains its stone rood screen survives as a ruin in the churchyard.

*** Denny Abbey** (Cambs.), Benedictine monks, Knights Templar and Franciscan nuns. A post-suppression farmhouse contains the substantial remains of the abbey church with evidence of all three groups of religious who settled the site. The refectory of the Franciscan nuns survives, converted to a barn. The extensive precinct of this impressive site is traceable by its earthworks.

Dorchester Abbey (Oxfordshire), Augustinian canons. Only the church, converted to parish use, survives.

*** Easby Abbey** (North Yorks.), Premonstratensian canons. The gatehouse and extensive claustral ranges survive as ruins, though the church has been substantially demolished, and the greater part of the precinct can be traced by its earthworks. The ruins of a service building, perhaps a barn, are incorporated in a largely modern house. The parish church, which pre-dates the abbey, survives within the precinct.

*** Egglestone Abbey** (Durham), Premonstratensian canons. The nave of the church and the east cloister range, converted to a post-suppression house, survive to roof height, the remainder of the church and cloister ranges being reduced to low walling. The extant buildings lie at the centre of a small precinct defined by earthworks.

Ford Abbey (Dorset), Cistercian monks. The south and east claustral ranges survive within an important sixteenth century mansion.

Fountains Abbey (North Yorks.), Cistercian monks. The largest monastic ruin in England, this site retains a substantially complete claustral nucleus, its mill, inner gatehouse and remains of inner and outer court buildings set within an extensive walled precinct.

*Furness Abbey (Cumbria), Savigniac, later Cistercian monks. The substantial ruins of the church, cloister buildings and a solitary service building lie within a well-preserved precinct still enclosed by a precinct wall with two gates. The gate-chapel and inner gatehouse also survive. Site Museum.

Garway Preceptory (Hereford and Worcester), Knights Templar, Knights Hospitlar. Only the dovecot built in 1326 by the Hospitlars survives.

*Gisborough Priory (Cleveland), Augustinian canons. Remains of the priory church, west cloister range and gatehouse. There is a remarkable collection of architectural fragments.

Glastonbury Abbey (Somerset), Benedictine monks. No trace of the Saxon monastery remains above ground, but of the post-conquest abbey there are remains of the church, cloister ranges, the remarkably complete abbot's kitchen, a precinct barn, precinct wall and gatehouse. Site Museum with a highly-detailed model.

*Gloucester Blackfriars (Glos.), Dominican friars. The church and cloister ranges remain substantially complete, retaining their medieval roofs and evidence for their post-suppression conversion to a mansion and factory.

Great Malvern Priory (Hereford and Worcester), Benedictine monks. Only the gatehouse and the priory church survive, the latter converted to parish use.

*Hailes Abbey (Glos.), Cistercian monks. Fragmentary remains of the church and cloister ranges at the centre of a well-preserved earthwork precinct. The gate-chapel survives as the parish church. Site Museum.

*Haughmond Abbey (Shropshire), Augustinian canons. Substantial remains of the cloister ranges and abbot's hall.

Horsham St Faith (Norfolk), Benedictine nuns. The refectory survives, converted to a post-suppression house, with the walls of the cloister enclosing its garden.

Humberston Abbey (Humberside), Benedictine monks. Only the west tower of the abbey church survives, the parochial nave being rebuilt in the eighteenth century. Partially excavated, a latrine block remains visible.

*Jarrow Priory (Tyne and Wear), Benedictine monks. Parts of the Saxon monastery church survive within the later church, which remains in use. The layout of the Saxon domestic buildings can still be seen below the ruins of post-conquest cloister ranges. Visitor Centre.

Jervaulx Abbey (North Yorks.), Cistercian monks. Substantial ruins of the cloister ranges within an early-nineteenth-century park that preserves the earthworks of the precinct. There are fragmentary ruins of the mill.

*Kirkham Priory (North Yorks.), Augustinian canons. Substantial ruins of the cloister buildings and a fine fourteenth-century gatehouse within an extensive precinct defined by earthworks.

Kirkstall Abbey (West Yorks.), Cistercian monks. Well-preserved ruins of the church and cloister buildings, the guest-house and inner gatehouse (converted to a house) within a landscaped park which has obscured the remainder of the precinct.

Kirkstead Abbey (Lincs.), Cistercian monks. The whole precinct of this untouched site is defined by impressive earthworks. A small fragment of the church survives, as does the gate-chapel, now the parish church.

Lacock Abbey (Wilts.), Augustinian canonesses. The cloister ranges and inner court survive as the shell of an important post-suppression mansion. The surrounding parkland contains some earthwork evidence of the medieval precinct.

*Lanercost Priory (Cumbria), Augustinian canons. The nave of the church remains in use, and the eastern arm and transepts though unroofed are tolerably complete. The east and south ranges of the cloister survive as ruins, and the west range containing the prior's apartments survives, converted to a post-suppression house. The present vicarage is in part medieval and may be the guest-house.

Lenton Priory (Nottinghamshire), Cluniac monks. The gate chapel and some small fragments of the church are all that survive.

Leominster Priory (Hereford and Worcester), Benedictine monks. The parochial nave of the priory church survives as the parish church.

Lewes Priory (Sussex), Cluniac monks. Parts of the east and south cloister ranges survive, including the substantial latrine block, as well as the western part of the church.

* Lilleshall Abbey (Shropshire), Augustinian canons. Substantial remains of the church and claustral ranges.

Lincoln Greyfriars (Lincs.), Franciscan friars. The two-storey south claustral range, of uncertain use, remains intact.

* Lindisfarne Priory (Northumberland), Benedictine monks. Substantial remains of the church, cloister ranges and inner court, but no trace of the pre-conquest monastery. Site Museum.

London Charterhouse (Greater London), Carthusian monks. Parts of the great cloister, church, chapter-house and lesser cloister survive amongst post-war buildings.

London Temple (Greater London), Knights Templar, later Knights Hospitlar. Only the church now survives.

Malmesbury Abbey (Wilts.), Benedictine monks. Only the nave and fragments of the crossing and south transept remain, the greater part of the nave serving as the parish church.

Maxstoke Priory (Warwicks.), Augustinian canons. The site of the church is marked by the fallen remains of its crossing tower at the centre of an extensive precinct defined by earthworks and a surviving precinct wall with a single gatehouse. The existing house contains the much altered remains of the prior's lodging and an inner gatehouse, and there are fragmentary remains of the infirmary.

Meaux Abbey (Humberside), Cistercian monks. The whole precinct is defined by well-preserved earthworks and a single surviving service building.

* Monk Bretton Priory (South Yorks.), Cluniac, later Benedictine monks. Extensive ruins of the church and cloister buildings. The west range survived as a post-suppression house (now ruined). The gatehouse survives, with two other buildings, the mill (converted to a house in the early seventeenth century) and an unidentified building in the inner court.

Monkwearmouth Priory (Tyne and Wear), Benedictine monks. Only the church which retains pre-conquest elements survives. Site Museum.

Mottisfont Priory (Hants.), Augustinian canons. The nave and crossing of the church survive within the sixteenth- and eighteenth-century mansion.

* Mount Grace Priory (North Yorks.), Carthusian monks. Substantial remains of the church, great and lesser cloisters, inner court, and outer court including fragments of the mill. Site Museum.

* Much Wenlock Priory (Shropshire), Cluniac monks. Ruins of the church and claustral ranges (including the prior's house and infirmary which survive within a post-suppression house) in the setting of a now largely destroyed nineteenth-century garden.

* Netley Abbey (Hants.), Cistercian monks. Well-preserved ruins of the church and claustral ranges set within parkland which retains some evidence of earthworks.

Newcastle Blackfriars (Tyne and Wear), Dominican friars. The cloister ranges survive with post-suppression modifications.

Norton Priory (Cheshire), Augustinian canons. The recently excavated church and cloister ranges are now displayed within parkland which retains evidence of the monastic precinct. Site Museum.

Pershore Abbey (Hereford and Worcester), Benedictine monks. The crossing, south transept and presbytery of the church survive as the parish church.

* Rievaulx Abbey (North Yorks.), Cistercian monks. Substantial ruins of the church and cloister ranges set within an extensive precinct defined by earthworks. Service buildings including a mill and the tannery survive, together with the gate-chapel.

* Roche Abbey (South Yorks.), Cistercian monks. The ruins of the church and cloister ranges lie at the centre of a precinct defined by a surviving wall and earthworks within late-eighteenth-century parkland.

Sandwell Priory (West Midlands), Benedictine monks. The excavated remains of the church and cloister ranges are displayed in a public park.

*Sawley Abbey (Lancs.), Cistercian monks. The ruins of the church and cloister ranges survive at the centre of a well-preserved earthwork precinct. One service building, perhaps a mill, survives, incorporated in modern housing.

Selby Abbey (North Yorks.), Benedictine monks. Only the church survives, functioning as the parish church.

*Shap Abbey (Cumbria), Premonstratensian canons. The ruins of the church and cloister ranges lie at the centre of a small precinct defined by earthworks.

Stamford, St Leonard's Priory (Lincs.), Benedictine monks. The nave of the priory church survives within a post-medieval barn.

Stanley Abbey (Wilts.), Cistercian monks. The precinct remains to a large extent identified by surviving earthworks.

Swine Priory (Humberside), Cistercian nuns. The eastern arm of the priory church survives in use by the parish. The remainder of the precinct that does not lie below modern farm buildings can be traced from earthworks.

Temple Bruer (Lincs.), Knights Templar, later Knights Hospitlar. All that now remains is the tower on the south side of the church, surrounded by modern farm buildings.

Thornholme Priory (Humberside), Augustinian canons. A substantially complete precinct is defined by earthworks and the ruins of a post-suppression farm.

*Thornton Abbey (Humberside), Augustinian canons. The greater part of the walled and moated precinct survives as earthworks centred on the slight ruins of the church and claustral buildings. The gatehouse is perhaps the finest monastic gatehouse to survive in England.

*Titchfield Abbey (Hants.), Premonstratensian canons. The nave of the church survives within the sixteenth-century gatehouse range of the post-suppression mansion. Much of the precinct, which contains an important barn, can be traced by its earthworks.

*Waltham Abbey (Essex), Augustinian canons. The parochial western part of the abbey church remains, together with the slight remains of the gatehouse and a fragment of the north cloister range.

Watton Priory (Humberside), Gilbertine nuns and canons. The priory church and nuns' cloister are traceable as earthworks, whilst the existing house is the prior's lodging. The canons' cloister buildings lie below its gardens. A derelict precinct barn survives.

*Waverley Abbey (Surrey), Cistercian monks. The slight ruins of the church and cloister ranges lie at the centre of a precinct which is partially traceable from its earthworks.

*Whitby Abbey (North Yorks.), Benedictine monks. Nothing is visible of the Saxon monastery buildings, though there are substantial ruins of the post-conquest church. The only other standing structure is a part of the abbot's house within the seventeenth–nineteenth-century Abbey House. The whole of the precinct can be traced from its earthworks, some elements of which are almost certainly pre-conquest.

Wilberfoss Priory (Humberside), Benedictine nuns. Only the nave of the priory church survives, still in the use of the parish.

Wymondham Abbey (Norfolk), Benedictine monks. The parochial nave and the ruined crossing are all that remain of this house apart from the earthworks of the buried cloister ranges.

York Abbey (North Yorks.), Benedictine monks. The whole of the precinct survives enclosed by a fortified precinct wall with three surviving gates. Within are the ruins of the church and east range (in the cellars of the Yorkshire Museum), the abbot's lodging (incorporated in the post-suppression King's Manor) and a much-restored guest hall. The remainder of the monastic buildings are buried below public gardens which are scattered with architectural fragments. Exhibition.

Further Reading

There is a considerable amount of literature on the subject of monasteries, most of it specific to individual sites. Remarkably, synthetic or critical works are hard to find. By far the best architectural overview can be found in R. Gilyard-Beer, *Abbeys, an Introduction* (London, HMSO, 1958). For a historian's perspective see C. P. S. Platt, *The Abbeys and Priories of Medieval England* (London 1984). The most recent archaeological opinions can be found in R. Gilchrist and H. Mytum (eds.), *The Archaeology of Rural Monasteries* British Archaeological Reports 203 (Oxford 1989). The last two have extensive bibliographies which include both general studies and discussions of individual sites.

For sites in the care of English Heritage, the National Trust and local authorities, informative and well-illustrated handbooks are generally available which often summarize more detailed studies and provide a good starting point. For more specialist readers, more detailed analysis is now becoming available for specific classes of monastery. For the Cistercians, see C. Norton and D. Park (eds.), *Cistercian Art and Architecture* (Cambridge 1986) and P. Fergusson, *The Architecture of Solitude* (Princeton 1984), and for the Augustinians, D. M. Robinson *The Geography of Augustinian Settlement in Medieval England and Wales*, British Archaeological Reports 80, vols. 1 & 2 (Oxford 1980).

Glossary

apse The rounded termination of a chapel, aisle or east end of a church or similar building, normally of eleventh- or twelfth-century date.

arcade A series of arches carried on columns, for instance between the main vessel of a church and an aisle, that carries the superstructure of the building.

bay The structural division of a building, normally emphasized in its architecture by vertical divisions, the placing of columns and buttresses.

bercary From the Latin *bercaria*, a monastic sheep ranch, signifying not simply buildings but also pastures and enclosures in open country.

bloomery A furnace for the smelting of iron ore.

buttress The localized widening of a wall at its bay divisions to provide additional support against the outward pressure exerted by roofs and vaults in a masonry building.

capital The decorative top to a column which carries the springing of the arches of an arcade, often highly carved and painted, or similarly the decorated top of a wall or nook-shaft.

carrels Individual desks, normally placed in one of the cloister alleys, and either of timber or stone construction, used for study and the copying of manuscripts.

cill-wall A narrow and low masonry wall provided for the support of a timber-framed structure to keep its lowest timber, the cill-beam, dry and free from rotting.

clerestory The upper storey of an aisled building, particularly a church, which was provided with windows to light the central vessel.

corbel A stone bracket, often carved, that projected from a wall-face to support timber-work, a wall-shaft or the ribs of a vault.

crenellation The appearance, real or imagined of fortification, normally in the form of battlements and turrets, and particularly applied to monastic gatehouses. A royal licence was required before any apparently defensible building could be erected.

crossing The point at which the principal axes of a cruciform church met at the junction of nave, presbytery and transepts. Normally it was architecturally marked by a tower, and it was the preferred location of the monks' choir stalls.

dendrochronology The dating of old timbers by the detailed study of their annual growth rings, which can establish a very close date for the felling of the tree used.

fother A late medieval measure of weight, approximately 19 hundredweight or a 'short ton', used almost exclusively for the quantifying of lead.

garth An enclosed yard or paddock, normally associated with particular buildings, for instance the bakehouse garth or stable garth.

guano Pigeon droppings collected for use in the tanning of parchment.

jamb The side of a door or window frame.

laver A washing place, normally placed in the cloister but also in the infirmary and other buildings, supplied with a piped water supply, and often distinguished by its architectural sophistication.

laybrother A monastic servant subject to the same discipline as the choir monks but unlettered and responsible for the day-to-day servicing of the community. They comprised the major element in early Cistercian monasteries where they were used to farm substantial estates, but most orders actually had them in small numbers.

nave   The central vessel of an aisled building. In the monastic church it signifies the long or western arm of the church which might be partly used by the laity or by laybrothers.

opus signinum   A hard and waterproof concrete, containing powdered brick or tile and consequently pink in colour. It was first used by the Romans.

pentice   A passage or corridor running along the side of a building, its single-pitch (or pent) roof being carried on corbels in the wall of that building. Such corridors were normally of light construction and have left little trace.

pier   A free-standing masonry column that supports an arcade.

presbytery   The eastern arm of a monastic church that contained the enclosure of the high altar to the east of the monks' choir stalls.

pulpitum   The screen that closed the west end of the monks' choir stalls, of either stone or timber.

quern   A hand-mill for the grinding of flour, often made of expensive imported lava.

respond   A half-pier placed against a wall at the end of an arcade.

rood screen   The screen that closes off the nave from the monks' part of the church, normally set directly to the east of the nave altar, with doors through it to either side of the altar. There was normally a loft over it which carried images of the Holy Virgin, St John and Christ crucified, which themselves constituted the 'rood'.

string-course   A horizontal moulding used to level up the coursing of rubble walls and to mark the structural divisions of elevations, for instance at window cill level or below a parapet.

transept   The north and south arms of a cruciform church to either side of the crossing, called the 'cross aisle' in medieval sources. They provided additional space for chapels.

transom   The horizontal division of lights in a multi-light window.

undercroft   A vaulted ground floor or semi-subterranean room, of secondary importance to the room above and often used only for storage.

vaccary   From the Latin *vaccaria*, a monastic cattle ranch, its buildings, paddocks and pastures.

vault   The fire-proof ceiling of a room constructed by turning arches of rubble stone set in mortar. Vaults vary greatly in complexity, from simple barrel vaults to elaborate ceilings divided into panels by decorative and moulded ribs.

Index